# Today's Teen

# Construction Skills

**Glencoe McGraw-Hill**

New York, New York    Columbus, Ohio    Woodland Hills, California    Peoria, Illinois

## Contributing Writers

Ann Price Gosch
Family and Consumer Sciences Educational Writer
Frequent contributor to *Sew News* magazine
Tacoma, Washington

Linda Turner Griepentrog
Editor, *Sew News*
Primedia
Golden, Colorado

Brenda Barrington Mendiola, M.S.
Home Economics Teacher
Irion County Schools
Mertzon, Texas

## Photo Credits

Liz Purcell          pp. 13-80, 93-95, 99, 100, 108-112

Gary Skillestad      pp. 82-92, 96-99, 102-107
— Art MacDillo's

*Glencoe/McGraw-Hill*

*A Division of The* **McGraw·Hill** *Companies*

Printed in the United States of America

Send all inquiries to:
Glencoe/McGraw-Hill
3008 W. Willow Knolls Drive
Peoria, IL 61614-1083

ISBN 0-07-820679-0

 2  3  4  5  6  7  8  9  10  **063**  04  03  02  01  00

# CONTENTS

# Serger Sewing

# Projects

## To the Teacher

*Today's Teen Construction Skills* includes reproducible Handouts covering conventional sewing, serger sewing, and projects suitable for beginning sewers. Much of the text material has been put into convenient Handouts that students can easily use at their sewing stations. The detailed illustrations help guide students through an array of sewing tasks.

# TEACHING CLOTHING

## Organizing the Clothing Lab

Effective organization in the clothing lab helps students successfully complete projects in the allotted time. Both teachers and students should be involved in arranging and maintaining materials, supplies, and equipment. Techniques for maximizing the use of both the material and the nonmaterial resources needed to complete sewing lab projects are included in this section.

## Tips for Assisting Students in Lab

One organizational problem frequently encountered when structuring a clothing lab is developing a procedure for assisting students when they need help. The procedure should be one that allows the teacher to easily see who needs help and then quickly and efficiently provide that help. The procedure should also allow a way for students to easily initiate a request for help while, at the same time, provide few opportunities for students to become disorderly. The procedure should also allow students to continue working while they are waiting for assistance.

The procedure selected is partially dependent on the number of students in the sewing lab. Following are suggestions for assisting both small and large lab groups.

## Small Groups (12 Students or Less)

Small groups allow the teacher to use less formality in the procedure for offering help to students than large groups since the teacher can possibly remember who has been assisted and who is next in line. However, to keep things running efficiently, it is a good idea to implement a set system. Some ideas that work well for small groups are described below. Any of the large group ideas could also be adapted for small groups.

1. Prepare a set of numbers on index cards—one number per card and at least one number for each student in the class. Students draw for a "help number" each day. Assist students in numerical order. Be sure to tell students that they cannot draw the same number every day.

2. Ask students to write their name on the board as they need help. The teacher then works around the room according to the list. Rules must be established regarding students erasing names or placing their own name above someone else's.

3. If the sewing machines are numbered, the teacher can routinely work through the numbers, alternating the pattern each day. One day might be 2, 4, 6, 8, the next 1, 3, 5, 7.

4. Students can make and decorate their own S.O.S. (Stuck on Something) flag from fabric or paper. These could be attached to dowel sticks and flown by standing them in a discarded serger cone placed at each machine.

## Large Groups (12 to 25 Students)

For larger groups of students, a variety of take-a-number ideas are offered. All involve some type of teacher-prepared tool. Most include materials commonly found in the classroom or inexpensively purchased from discount stores. All require students to take a number, with the teacher assisting in numerical order. If the class period ends before all students are assisted, the teacher should begin the next day with those who were not assisted the day before.

1. Prepare a set of small numbered sandwich-board cards students may pick up from a designated place and take to their machines as they need help. The cards should be returned to their designated place and replaced in numerical order as each student is assisted.

2. Clothespins could be numbered and clipped in numerical order along the bottom of a poster board. The names of students should be written down the side of the poster. As students need help, they take a numbered clothespin and clip it to their name. The pin is returned to the bottom of the poster after the student has been assisted.

3. Prepare a set of numbered flags mounted in weighted cans or cups that students can pick up from a designated place to fly at their machine as a signal for help. The flags are to be returned to the designated spot after assistance.

4. If there is access to a bulletin board in the sewing area, student names could be listed down one side on colorful construction paper. A circle of self-stick hook and loop tape should be placed after each name. A set of numbered large circles with hook and loop fastener circles on the back should be placed in numerical order on a strip of hook and loop tape along the bottom of the bulletin board. As a student needs help, he or she removes a numbered circle from the bottom strip and places it by his or her name. The circles are returned to the bottom strip after the student is assisted. The tape can be stapled to the bulletin board for extra stability.

5. Large numbered cards placed on ribbons could be prepared for students to wear around their necks when they have questions. These could be hung on a pegboard hook in the sewing area. A variation would be to make large numbered buttons for students to wear indicating that they need assistance.

In both small and large groups, the teacher may find that a few students always seem to require more attention than other students. One way to deal with this is to give each student two or three colored tokens or chips each day. As the student is assisted, he or she turns in a chip. When he or she runs out of chips, he or she will have to wait for assistance until all other students have been helped. To encourage sewing independence, require students to circle the area on the guide sheet that is causing them problems and to formulate a question to clarify the problem. This ensures that students read instructions and try to interpret them before asking for assistance.

## Choosing Projects

A second organizational problem that often occurs in clothing lab classes involves considerations for choosing projects appropriate for all students. Begin by deciding who will select the project.

Teacher-selected projects may not create the excitement that student-selected projects do. Students should have some voice in selecting the project, especially if they will be required to pay for it. If students are allowed to choose, guidelines concerning fabric and pattern types suitable should be given.

The advantage of a teacher-selected project is that the teacher has some control over the degree of difficulty of the projects selected. Cost can also be somewhat controlled. Teacher-selected projects tend to be similar in nature. The drawback is that students may not be excited about a project that looks like everyone else's. This is especially true if the project is a garment. This problem can be eliminated by selecting a garment that can have slight variations or embellishments so that the finished product is personalized in some way.

Whether the project is teacher- or student-selected, the following factors must be considered:
1. Number of students per class
2. Student ability levels
3. Amount of time allotted
4. Ratio of students to equipment
5. Project cost

### Number of Students

Large groups of students need simple projects that are similar in nature, particularly if most of the students are beginners. This allows the teacher to direct his or her attention to groups rather than individuals. Small groups can have more variety and more difficult projects.

### Ability Level—Beginning

When teaching beginning sewing students, it is easiest to have students working on similar projects. This allows the teacher to demonstrate and the students to mirror the teacher and each other. For these classes, the teacher might want to order prepackaged sewing kits or make sewing kits for each student. Most prepackaged kits contain the fabric, thread, pattern and other supplies needed to complete a project—all for a nominal fee. The teacher should check the quality of kits beforehand. Some kits require extra items, such as stuffing for pillows, to be purchased.

If the teacher chooses to make kits for each student, the kits should contain fabric, pattern, thread, and supplies necessary for completing the project. These items could be purchased from class funds or charged to each student.

## Ability Level—Advanced

In a more advanced class where students may be allowed to choose their own projects, students could be partnered with someone making a similar project. This allows students to assist each other when the teacher is not immediately available. Advanced students benefit from the opportunity to select a project of their own, requiring them to apply critical thinking skills in order to complete their project.

## Ability Level—Mixed

The more advanced students in a class with beginning students may not be challenged by a beginning level project. When there are multiple levels of sewers in one class, students may benefit from being grouped by ability. Projects in each group may need to be similar. Another option would be to group beginning sewers with advanced sewers to encourage peer tutoring.

## Amount of Time Allotted

Projects that must be completed in a short period of time should all be similar and should be simpler than those stretched out over several weeks. For example: a stuffed pillow could be completed in a few class periods; a fitted shirt with collar, cuffs, and front band could not.

## Ratio of Students to Equipment

Students who must share machines can benefit from being partnered with someone sewing a similar project because they may be able to keep the same stitch length, machine settings, and thread as their partner. Students can also benefit from cooperative problem solving when they work with a partner or partners.

If there are more than two students per machine, students might be placed on a rotation schedule to ensure that all students have equal time on the machines. Selecting a project that includes decorative hand sewing or embellishments on it will give students something to work on when they are not sewing on the machine.

## Project Cost

In these challenging economic times, teachers need to take the cost of projects into consideration when planning student projects. If you are preparing kits, keep the cost low to moderate. If students are choosing their own projects, encourage them to choose items that fit their personal or family budget.

A dilemma that faces many teachers is what to do with a student who has no funds for a project. Many teachers find it helpful to allocate some funds in the department budget for items, such as placemats and napkins, that students could make for the school at no cost to themselves.

# Equipment

Equipment may vary somewhat from classroom to classroom. In general, use the following guidelines in determining what equipment to have in the classroom.

## Student Equipment

In order to make sure that each student has the minimal sewing equipment necessary to complete a project, classroom sewing kits should be purchased if funds allow. Classroom kits assure uniformity in equipment and supplies from student to student. Each kit should contain the following items:

1. Bent-handled dressmaker's shears: 7- to 8-inch (18 to 20 cm)
2. Cutting scissors: 5- to 6-inch (12 to 15 cm) for clipping threads, cutting patterns, trimming, and grading seams, etc.
3. Sewing or hem gauge: 6-inch (15 cm) with slide marker
4. Tape measure: 60-inch (152 cm) with numbers on both sides
5. Dressmaker's chalk pencil: white and blue
6. Pincushion with pins: preferably stainless steel, ¼ inch (3.2 cm) pins with colored plastic balls on the ends
7. Seam ripper: sharp, with a cover

A plastic school box, zipper bag, or basket should be placed at each sewing machine to hold these basic pieces of equipment. Each machine should have a number taped to it. Use tape or permanent markers to label each piece of equipment with the same number as the machine to which it is assigned. If students are sharing machines, kits can be shared or more than one kit per machine can be prepared. In such cases, equipment could be numbered 1A, 1B, etc.

The kits can either be checked in and out daily or allowed to remain at each machine throughout the sewing lab. Students could be asked to put up a deposit in order to initially receive their kit. The deposit would then be returned when they turn in their kit. Students could also be required to replace or pay for items that disappear from their supply kits.

If funds are not available and students will be required to purchase or bring their own sewing supplies, the same items as those listed previously should be required. Another option is to purchase prepackaged kits available at fabric and discount stores. These can be sold to students at minimal cost. This would allow students to take a sewing kit home, which might encourage them to sew at home.

When departmental funds are low, one way to obtain individual classroom sewing kits is to build them up from year to year. Buying one or two items each year results in building complete kits over a period of time, without requiring a large initial investment.

In addition to the equipment in these kits, each student should have access to the following items:

## Measuring Tools
- Transparent ruler
- Measuring stick
- Retractable tape measure

## Marking Tools
- Tailor's chalk in a variety of colors
- Fabric markers
- Tracing wheels—serrated edge and smooth edge
- Tracing paper in a variety of colors as well as the type that disappears

## Cutting Tools
- Left-handed bent-handle dressmaker's shears, 7- to 8-inch (18 to 20 cm)
- Pinking shears both left and right handed
- Left-handed small cutting scissors, 5- to 6-inch (12 to 15 cm)
- Buttonhole scissors
- Small rotary cutter, plastic mat, and weights

## Pins, Needles, and Pincushions
- Sharps (hand sewing needles) sizes 1 to 12 (7 and 8 are the most common)
- Regular machine needles, from very fine U.S. size 10 (European size 70) to U.S. size 14 (European size 90). Ballpoint sewing machine needles in these same sizes are available for knits. Universal needles (used for woven or knit fabrics) might also be useful.
- Thimbles, in a variety of sizes
- Needle threader
- Tomato pincushion with emery pack
- Magnetic pin catcher

## Tools for Machine Maintenance
- Small brush
- Machine oil
- Small screwdrivers
- Pressurized canned air

## Serger Supplies
- Tweezers
- Needle grippers or pliers
- Needle threader
- Looper threader
- Pressurized canned air for cleaning
- Waste container
- Lint brush
- Industrial machine needles, U.S. sizes 10 to 16 (European sizes 70 to 100); or conventional needles, U.S. sizes 10 to 18 (European sizes 70 to 110)
- Ballpoint needles for knit fabric
- Cone adapters

- Spool caps to keep thread flowing smoothly from conventional spools
- Thread nets to keep decorative threads unwinding smoothly
- Seam sealant
- Loop turner, knit picker, latch hook or crochet hook for securing seam ends
- Foot pedal mat
- Serger blades or knives
- Rolled hem attachment
- Blind hem foot
- Elastic foot
- Tape guide for applying elastic ribbons or trims for fabric edges

### Pressing Equipment

- Steam iron
- Distilled water
- Measuring cup
- Iron cleaner
- Press cloth
- Ironing board, pad, and cover
- Sleeve board
- Tailor's ham
- Seam roll
- Press mitt

## Classroom Arrangement

In addition to the small sewing equipment that should be available in the sewing lab, the sewing facility should be furnished with the following:

- Tables for layout and cutting, preferably 35 inches (89 cm) high and at least 40 inches (101.5 cm) wide and 72 inches (183 cm) long. Those with storage bins on the end that fold up smaller for storage are ideal.
- Trays for storage of student projects
- Storage for hanging items
- Storage for patterns, fabric, small equipment, and supplies

- Full-length, three-way mirror
- Private dressing area
- Thread and cone rack
- Pant press
- Adequate lighting
- At least one machine and cabinet for each two students
- One chair per student
- Serger machines

Sewing machines should be arranged with safety in mind. The first consideration is the location of electrical outlets. Machines should be arranged so that cords do not cross traffic patterns. The cords should also be kept free of machine needles. Avoid overloading outlets and using extension cords. See the Handout "Sewing Safely" on page 10 for additional safety tips.

## Evaluation

Evaluation in the clothing lab needs to be more than just a single final project grade that focuses only on the finished product. Daily or weekly checks allow for evaluation of the process on a consistent and continual basis. Both the student and teacher should be involved in the evaluation process. The "Daily Lab Evaluation" on page 11 can be used by both the teacher and student as an evaluation of daily progress. The "Project Evaluation" Handout on page 12 can be used by both the student and teacher as each project step is completed. A variety of evaluation methods should be used throughout the course. Students should be aware of when they are being evaluated and should be familiar with the evaluation tools being used.

# SEWING SAFELY

## Preventing Falls

- Pick up dropped objects from floor immediately.
- Use a sturdy ladder or step stool for reaching high places. It is unsafe to stand on folding chairs, desks, boxes, or crates.
- Keep cabinet doors and drawers closed.
- Position cords so they won't be tripped over.

## Preventing Electrical Shock

- Plug the cord into the machine and foot control *before* plugging into the electrical outlet. Disconnect the cord from the electrical outlet first, then from the machine and foot control.
- Make sure all surfaces are dry before plugging in the machine.
- Keep electrical cords away from machine needles and cutting tools.

## Preventing Cuts

- When handing scissors or seam rippers to a classmate, make sure you extend the handles rather than the points.
- Keep protective sheaths on scissors and seam rippers when not in use.
- Do not walk around with scissors or seam rippers out of their protective sheaths.

## Preventing Needle and Pin Injuries

- Never hold needles or pins in your mouth.
- Use the appropriate needle size and type for the fabric you are sewing whether sewing by hand or by machine.
- Replace needles often to prevent breakage.
- Keep needles and pins in pincushions or on magnetic pin catchers when not in use. Pins kept in boxes spill easily.

- Never sew over needles or pins when using the sewing machine.
- Position fingers so that they are away from the machine needle.
- Avoid pulling or pushing the fabric through the machine when sewing to prevent needle breakage.
- Use the handwheel to guide the needle through thick seams.
- Make sure the needle is out of the fabric before removing fabric from the machine or changing the stitch controls.
- Make sure the machine is turned off or unplugged when making repairs, changing needles, or cleaning the machine.

## Preventing Burns and Electrical Shock While Using an Iron

- Plug the iron into the electrical outlet before turning the iron on. Turn the iron off before removing the plug from the electrical outlet to prevent electrical shocks.
- Position the iron cord so that it cannot be tripped over.
- Before filling a steam iron with water, make sure it is turned off and unplugged.
- Beware of steam coming from the iron. Keep hands, fingers, and other body parts away from the iron's heat source.
- Place the iron on its heel when it is not in use.
- Be sure to turn the iron off and then unplug it when you are through using it.
- Empty any remaining water from the iron after it has been unplugged and cooled.
- Store the iron only after it has completely cooled.

Name_____ Date _____ Class_____

# DAILY LAB EVALUATION

**Directions:** Read each statement below. Then answer "Yes" or "No" as it applies to the work you completed in sewing lab today. Have your teacher verify your responses. Then total the number of "Yes" and "No" responses from the two columns in the space provided.

| Statement | Teacher Response | Student Response |
|---|---|---|
| 1. Started on time; used time in class wisely. | | |
| 2. Worked quietly without being disruptive. | | |
| 3. Read and attempted to interpret instructions before asking questions. | | |
| 4. Used sewing and pressing equipment in a safe manner. | | |
| 5. Kept sewing materials and supplies organized and neat. | | |
| 6. Had all sewing supplies and materials needed. | | |
| 7. Worked on project until instructed to put things away. | | |
| 8. Maintained a positive attitude about the sewing machine and sewing. | | |
| 9. Worked with the teacher and classmates in a courteous and respectful manner. | | |
| 10. Left sewing area neat when class ended. | | |

**Scale**
18–20 Yes = A
16–17 Yes = B
14–15 Yes = C
12–13 Yes = D
Below 12 Yes = F

Total "Yes" Points = _____

Total "No" Points = _____

## Handout 3

# PROJECT EVALUATION

**Directions:** Rate each step as you complete it using the following scale: 5 = Excellent; 4 = Good; 3 = Average; 2 = Fair; 1 = Poor. Have your teacher respond after you have completed your evaluation. Then total the points in the space provided at the bottom of the page.

| Teacher | Student | Evaluation Standards |
|---|---|---|
| | | **Pattern Layout and Pinning** <br> A. Pins are placed diagonally at corners and perpendicular to seamlines. |
| | | B. Pin points are facing the cutting line and placed inside the stitching line. |
| | | C. Pattern is smooth, with adequate pins at fold lines, grainline arrows, corners, and notches. |
| | | D. Pattern pieces are placed according to pattern layout instructions. |
| | | **Cutting** <br> A. On straight edges, cutting is done with shears, using long firm strokes along the cutting line. |
| | | B. On curved areas, cutting is done with shears, using short strokes along the cutting line. |
| | | C. Notches are cut so that they protrude on the outside of the cutting line. |
| | | D. Fabric is cut flat without lifting it from the cutting surface. |
| | | **Marking** <br> A. Correct symbols are transferred from the pattern to the fabric. |
| | | B. The marking method selected is appropriate for the pattern and the fabric. |
| | | C. Marking isn't visible on the outside of the project. |
| | | **Sewing** <br> A. Seams are sewn with fabric placed right sides together. |
| | | B. Seams are straight on the ⅝-inch (1.6 cm) seamline. |
| | | C. The correct stitch length for the fabric is used. |
| | | D. The seams are clipped or notched where needed in order to lie flat. |
| | | **Finishing** <br> A. Appropriate seam finish is used on all seams. |
| | | B. Loose and hanging threads have been clipped off close to the fabric. |
| | | C. The garment or project is well pressed. |

_____ Total Points (Teacher, 90 possible)

_____ Total Points (Student, 90 possible)

**Handout 4**

# HOW TO ALTER YOUR PATTERN

Follow these guidelines for successful pattern alterations:
- Adjustments for length and width must be made on both front and back pattern pieces.
- A width adjustment of 2 inches (5 cm) or less can be made along the side seams of a garment.
- Check to make sure the grainline remains straight.
- Redraw any design details or darts changed by the pattern alteration.
  The following illustrations and directions tell about some common pattern adjustments.

## Lengthening a Pattern

1. Cut the pattern apart on the adjustment lines.
2. Tape tissue paper to one pattern piece.
3. Using a measuring stick, extend the grainline by drawing one continuous straight line through the tissue paper.
4. Measure down the amount needed for length. Tape the second piece of the pattern to the tissue paper at that point, making sure the grainlines match up.
5. Connect the cutting lines.
6. Use the same method to adjust the back pattern piece.

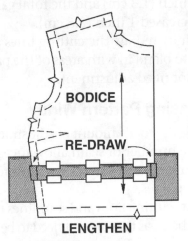

LENGTHEN

Lengthening the pattern.

## Shortening a Pattern

1. Measure the amount to be shortened upwards from the adjustment line on the front pattern piece.
2. At that point, draw a second line that is parallel to the adjustment line.
3. Fold the pattern along the adjustment line and bring it down so that the adjustment line now lies directly over the line you drew in Step 2. Match the grainline markings. Tape the fold in place.
4. Use the same method to adjust the back pattern piece.

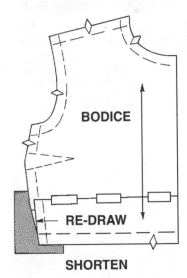

SHORTEN

Shortening the pattern.

Continued on next page

## Increasing Pattern Width

1. Tape tissue paper along the pattern piece edge.
2. Divide the total adjustment needed by the number of seam allowances. If a garment has two side seams and four seam allowances, the amount to be adjusted on each piece is one-fourth the total amount.
3. Measure the amount needed outward from the cutting lines. For example, to increase the waist-line by 1 inch (2.5 cm), add ¼ inch (6 mm) to the side seam of the front pattern piece and ¼ inch (6 mm) to the side seam of the back pattern piece. Both side seams will be increased by ½ inch (1.3 cm) and the total garment will be increased 1 inch (2.5 cm).
4. Carefully redraw the cutting lines and seamlines to blend in with areas of the pattern that did not need adjustment.

## Decreasing Pattern Width

1. Divide the total amount of adjustment needed by the number of seam allowances.
2. Measure the amount needed inward from the cutting lines.
3. Redraw cutting lines and seamlines to blend in with the areas that did not need to be decreased.

**SKIRT FRONT**

**INCREASE**

Increasing the pattern.

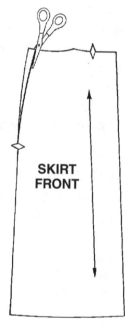

**SKIRT FRONT**

**DECREASE**

Decreasing the pattern.

## Handout 5

# PATTERN LAYOUT

To prepare your pattern for layout, follow these steps:

1. Cut apart the pattern pieces you need. To avoid accidentally trimming away the cutting lines, leave some extra paper outside the cutting lines on all pieces.
2. Check off the pattern pieces needed as you find them. Place the extra pieces back into the envelope.
3. Iron pattern pieces with a warm, dry iron.
4. Write your name on the pattern pieces.

## Positioning the Pattern Pieces

1. Find and circle the correct layout on your pattern guide sheet.
2. Check the layout instructions carefully. Note the following markings:
   - right and wrong sides of the fabric
   - right and wrong sides of the pattern (usually indicated by shaded pattern pieces on the layout)
   - pattern pieces to be cut a second time
   - any pieces to be cut from a single layer of fabric
3. Fold the fabric as shown in the layout diagram. If your fabric is longer than your work table, don't let it hang over the ends of the table. Keep extra fabric folded at the end of the table until it is needed.
4. Carefully place the pattern pieces on the fabric as shown. Use your eyes to line up the grainline arrows with the grain of the fabric, or place the piece on the fold if the pattern has the "fold" symbol on it. Use one or two pins to secure each piece. After you have pinned on a pattern piece, check it off on the guide sheet.

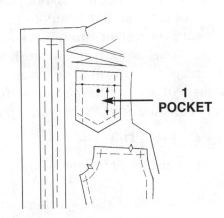

Step 1: Cutting apart pattern pieces.

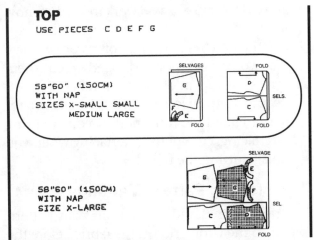

Step 1: Finding the correct layout on your pattern guide sheet.

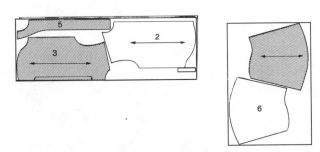

Step 2: Layout on single layers of fabric.

Continued on next page

5. Pin each pattern piece securely to the fabric, checking grainlines. Start with large pattern pieces placed on the fold. Pin securely, smoothing out the pattern as you go.

6. Pin the remaining pattern pieces so the grainline symbol is straight on the fabric grain. Pin one end of the grainline symbol to the fabric. Measure the distance from that end of the arrow to the selvage. Then measure from the other end of the arrow to the selvage. If the measurements are not the same, move the pattern until they are. Smooth the pattern and pin.

## Cutting Out the Pattern

1. Cut out your fabric, following the outside edges of the cutting lines carefully. Do not cut on the fold line. Hold the pattern and fabric flat with one hand as you cut with the other to prevent the layers from shifting. Move around the table as you work instead of moving the fabric.

2. Cut the notches outward, not inward. If there are two or three notches together, cut them across the top, as one long notch.

3. Keep pattern pieces pinned to the fabric for marking and identification. If you are using interfacing, cut out the interfacing when you finish cutting the fabric.

## Transferring Pattern Markings

Transfer lines and symbols on your pattern pieces to the wrong side of the fabric before the pattern is unpinned. Here are some methods for marking your fabric:

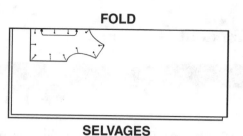

**FOLD**

**SELVAGES**

Step 5: Pin pattern pieces securely.

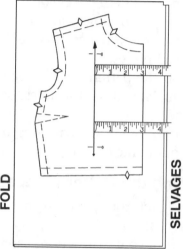

FOLD

SELVAGES

Step 6: Measuring the grainline.

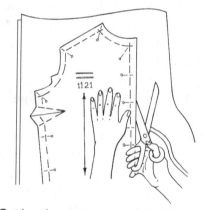

Step 1: Cutting the pattern out of the fabric.

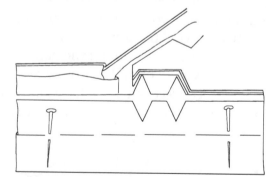

Step 2: Cut notches outward, not inward.

Continued on next page

## Tracing Paper and Wheel

1. Choose a color of tracing paper that can be easily seen, but is close to the color of your fabric. Slide the tracing paper under the pattern so that the colored side is against the wrong side of the fabric. If you need to mark two layers of fabric, use two sheets of tracing paper.
2. Roll the tracing wheel along the necessary markings. Using a ruler will help keep the lines straight. Mark the dots with an "X."

## Chalk and Pins

1. Put a pin through the pattern and the fabric at the place to be marked.
2. Make a chalk mark on the wrong side of both fabric layers at the pin marking.

## Washable Fabric Markers

1. Test markers on a scrap of fabric to be sure the markings can be removed.
2. Follow the directions for "Chalk and Pins."

## Thread Markings

1. Use a double strand of contrasting, light color thread. Do not knot the end.
2. With the point of your needle, tear a small hole in the pattern tissue at the mark to be transferred.
3. Take a single small stitch through the tissue and fabric. Leave a long tail, about 2 inches (5 cm). Then take another stitch in the same place to form a large loop. Clip threads, leaving another long tail.
4. Carefully remove the pattern tissue.
5. Pull the layers apart gently and clip the thread between them to leave short lengths in each layer. (If you're marking only one layer, just cut through the top of the loop.)

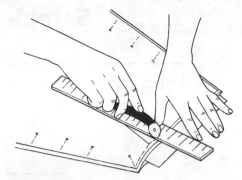

Step 2: Using a tracing wheel to transfer markings.

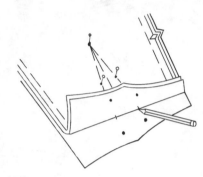

Step 2: Marking with a chalk pencil or washable fabric marker.

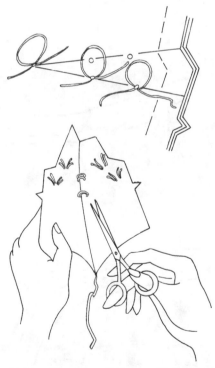

Step 3: Making thread markings or "tailor's tacks."

Continued on next page

**TODAY'S TEEN CONSTRUCTION SKILLS** **17**

# Sample Bodice Pattern

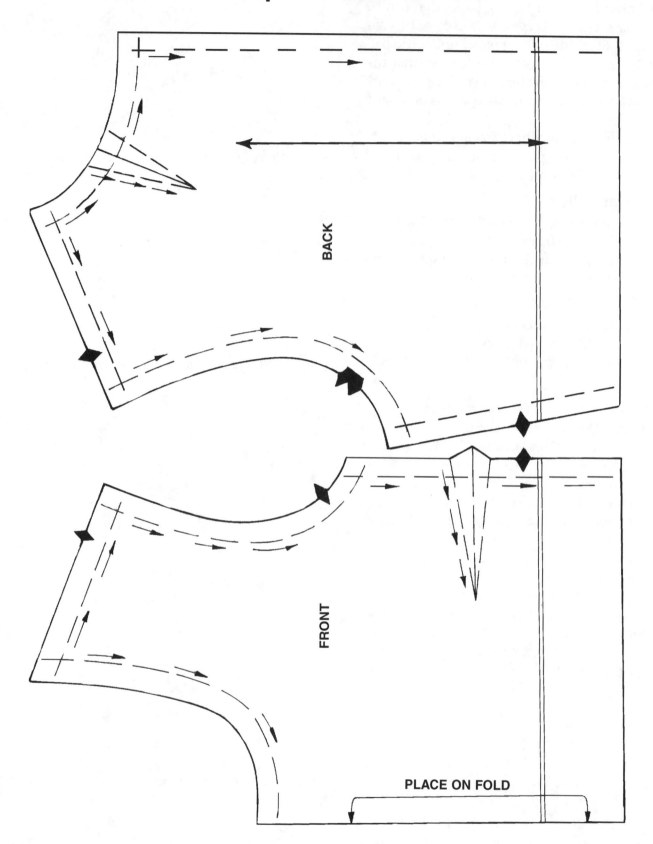

BACK

FRONT

PLACE ON FOLD

**Handout 6**

# PRESSING AND IRONING

Pressing should not be confused with ironing. *Pressing* is an up-and-down motion; the iron is lowered onto an area of the garment and then raised, then lowered onto the next area and raised, and so on. *Ironing* is gliding the iron back and forth over the fabric.

1. Press from the wrong side of the fabric whenever possible. That way all seams can be seen clearly and pressed correctly.

2. Sometimes you can't press on the wrong side because the seams or garment sections are enclosed, as with patch pockets. When working from the right side, use a press cloth to prevent overpressing or a shiny mark on the fabric. A piece of lightweight fabric such as batiste, organdy, or cheesecloth works well. For fabrics with a nap, such as velveteen or corduroy, use a piece of the same fabric. Place the two naps face to face to prevent the nap from becoming crushed and prevent press marks on the fabric.

3. Never press over pins because they will leave an impression on your fabric and scratch your iron.

4. Be cautious when pressing over basting—it can leave marks on your fabric. Always use white or light color thread for basting because the steam may release the dye from the thread, which will mark your fabric.

5. Use the correct heat setting for your fabric. First test the iron on a scrap of the fabric. If the scrap seems to stick, melt, pucker, or create smoke, the iron is much too hot. Synthetic fibers tend to be quite sensitive to heat, so set the iron on cooler settings.

6. Always press seams and darts before other seams are stitched across them. This helps reduce bulk and prevents a lumpy appearance in the finished garment.

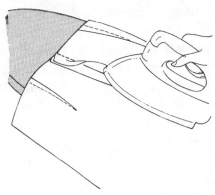

Step 6: Pressing seams and darts reduces bulk and prevents a lumpy appearance.

Continued on next page

7. Check the fit of the garment before you press any sharp creases such as pleats.

8. Always press seams flat first, before you press them open. This allows the stitches to settle into the fabric before the seam is pressed open. It's a good way to eliminate puckers on seams that do not appear flat.

9. Enclosed seams, such as those on collars and lapels, should also be pressed flat first, then pressed open before the garment section is turned right side out. Careful pressing in this way allows the seams to fall sharply along the edge of the finished garment. Press enclosed seams with the tip of your iron or use a point presser to get to hard-to-reach areas.

10. Use the tip of your iron to press only the seam-line itself if the fabric is likely to show pressing marks on the right side of the garment. Place a strip of brown paper cut from a grocery bag under the seam allowances as you press to avoid pressing an indentation into the outer fabric.

11. Press curved seams and darts over a curved surface such as a pressing mitt or tailor's ham.

12. When ironing or pressing garments, avoid wrinkling parts that have already been ironed. Start with small sections of the garment, such as detail areas, and work up to the largest sections. After ironing the garment, touch up important parts, if necessary.

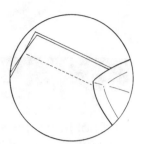

Step 8: Press the seam flat first.

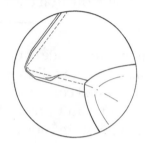

Step 9: Pressing an enclosed seam.

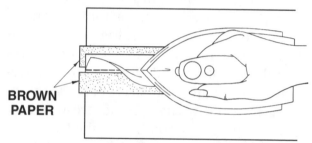

BROWN PAPER

Step 10: Use strips of brown paper under seam allowances to prevent indentations from the seams.

Step 11: Ironing a curved area with a tailor's ham.

Continued on next page

## Ironing a Shirt

1. Hang the shirt from one shoulder over the narrow end of the ironing board. Iron the shoulder area. Repeat for the other shoulder.
2. Iron the cuffs.
3. Iron the collar and neckband flat until they are smooth and crisp. If necessary, hold the collar taut with one hand as you iron.
4. Lay out one sleeve on the ironing board with the cuff opening up. Fold the sleeve with the underarm seam on the edge of the fold and smooth out the sleeve. Iron the sleeve flat, but not the cuff. Use the point of the iron to press neatly around the cuff opening and any tucks where the sleeve joins the cuff. Turn the sleeve over and lightly iron the other side, if necessary.
5. Repeat for the other sleeve. Keep the ironed sleeve out of the way to avoid wrinkling it.
6. Place one side of the shirt front opening on the narrow end of the ironing board. Iron the front edge to make it smooth and crisp.
7. Move the shirt around the board to iron the side, back, other side, and other front of the shirt. Use the point of the iron to press around buttons.
8. Touch up the collar if necessary. To avoid wrinkling the shirt, lay the collar on the edge of the ironing board with the shirt hanging off the edge.

Step 1: Iron the shoulder area of a shirt first.

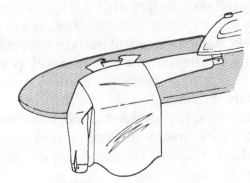

Step 4: Ironing sleeves.

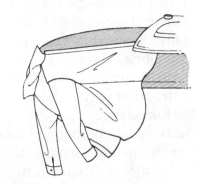

Step 6: Ironing the front of the shirt.

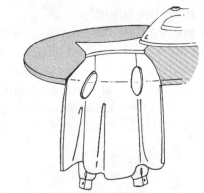

Step 8: Touch up the collar last.

Handout 7

# SEWING DARTS

Stitch darts before the seams are sewn, as follows:

1. Fold the fabric (right sides together) on the center line of the dart. Pin baste on the stitching line, carefully matching the lines accurately. Place the heads of the pins toward the point of the dart for easy removal as you stitch. For extra accuracy, press along the fold before stitching.

2. Stitch from the wide end to the point. Backstitch to secure the stitching at the wide end of the dart. Follow the stitching line, removing the pins as you sew.

   *Note:* Double-point darts have two pointed ends. On these contour darts, start at the center and stitch to each point. Some contour darts require clipping to prevent puckering.

3. To prevent bubbles and give a smooth point to your darts, gradually curve your stitching line near the point so that the final stitches are on the folded edge.

4. Secure the threads at the point of the dart by tying them together. Place a pin at the point of the dart to control the knot. The threads will slide down the pin and tighten at the point of the dart. Clip the thread ends to ¼ inch (6 mm) from the fabric.

5. Always press a dart before you sew over it with another seam. First, press it flat as stitched. Then press it to one side over a tailor's ham or pressing mitt to shape the garment. Press underarm darts toward the waistline. Press all other darts toward the center of the garment.

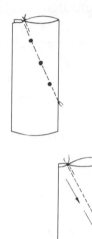

Step 1: Single-pointed dart, pinned and ready to sew.

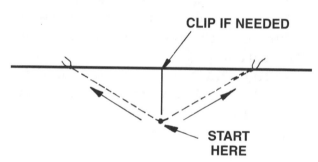

**CLIP IF NEEDED**

**START HERE**

Step 2: Stitching a double-pointed dart.

Continued on next page

Name_____ Date_____ Class_____

# Sample Dart Patterns

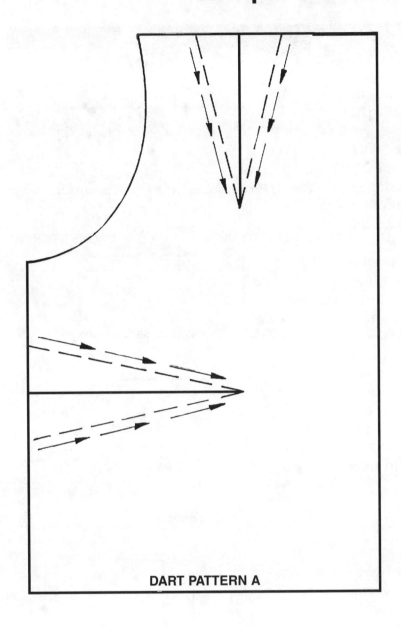

**DART PATTERN A**

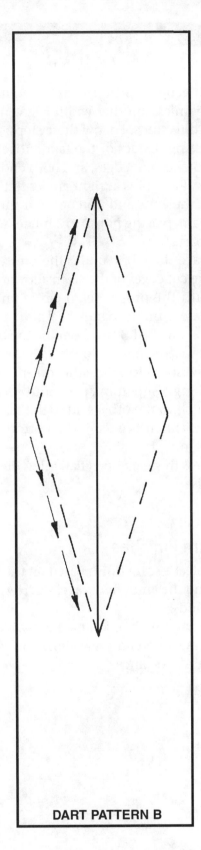

**DART PATTERN B**

## Handout 8

# SEWING SEAMS AND SEAM FINISHES

In general, plain seams are ⅝ inch (1.6 cm) wide unless another width is given in the pattern directions. Follow these steps:

1. Put right sides of the fabric together. Match notches, cut edges, and both ends of the fabric. Place pins at right angles to the seamline at the ends and notches. Pin the rest of the seam, placing pins 2 to 3 inches (5 to 7.5 cm) apart.
2. Place the fabric under the presser foot with the cut edges of the seam allowance lined up with the proper seam guide on the throat plate. Turn the handwheel and insert the needle ½ inch (1.3 cm) from the top of the fabric. Lower the presser foot.
3. Backstitch to secure the top end of the seam.
4. Using a medium speed and an even pace, stitch to the other end of the seam.
5. Backstitch to secure the bottom end of the seam.
6. Press the seam open flat unless directed otherwise.

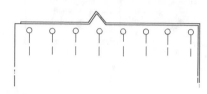

Step 1: Pinning seams together with notches matching.

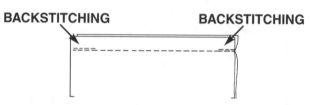

Steps 3 and 5: Backstitch to secure seam ends.

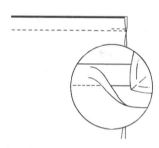

Step 6: Pressing the seam.

## Seam Finishes

Select a seam finish based on the type of fabric and the amount of raveling. Here are several methods:

• **Zigzag finish.** Use a medium-width machine zigzag stitch and sew along the edge of each seam allowance.

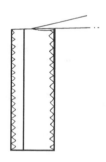

Zigzag finish.

Continued on next page

- **Overcast finish.** Stitch at a slant by hand with large, even, closely-spaced stitches that go over and around the edge of the fabric.
- **Clean finish.** Machine stitch ¼ inch (6 mm) from the cut edge. Turn the cut edge toward the inside along the stitching line. Press. Machine stitch close to the folded edge.
- **Serged finish.** Serge along the cut edge of the seam, trimming ⅛ inch (3 mm) or less as you sew.

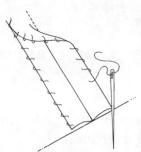

Overcast finish.

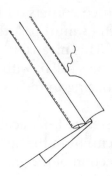

Clean finish.

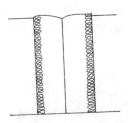

Serged finish.

# INTERFACING

To apply sew-on or fusible interfacing, use the following directions.

## Applying Sew-On Interfacing

1. Cut the pointed corners off the interfacing about ⅛ inch (3 mm) past the seamline to reduce bulk. This means ⅛ inch (3 mm) of the fabric corners will be without interfacing.
2. Pin the interfacing to the wrong side of the fabric piece.
3. Machine baste the interfacing to the fabric ½ inch (1.3 cm) from the outer edges. Stitch with the direction of the grain.
4. Trim the interfacing as close to the stitching line as possible.
5. Handle the interfacing and the fabric as one piece when sewing the seams.

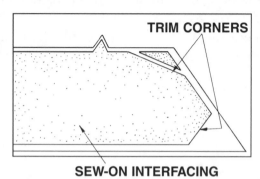

Step 1: Trimming sew-on interfacing before pinning to the fabric.

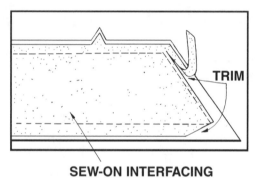

Step 4: Trimming sew-on interfacing close to the stitching line.

## Applying Fusible Interfacing

1. Trim fusible interfacing before it is pressed onto the fabric. Mark and trim ½ inch (1.3 cm) along the seamlines. Also, cut any pointed corners off the interfacing about ⅛ inch (3 mm) past the seamline to reduce bulk.
2. Place the coated side of the interfacing on the wrong side of the fabric. Be sure the cut edges are ½ inch (1.3 cm) from the fabric edges.
3. Fuse the interfacing in position, following the instructions that come with the interfacing.

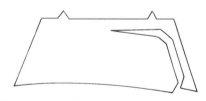

Step 1: Trimming fusible interfacing.

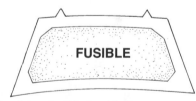

Step 2: Applying fusible interfacing.

## Handout 10

# GRADING, CLIPPING, NOTCHING, AND UNDERSTITCHING FACINGS

Follow these steps to help enclosed seams lie flat and smooth:

## Grading Seams

Trim the interfacing as close as possible to the seamline; trim the facing seam to ¼ inch (6 mm); then trim the garment seam to ⅜ inch (1 cm). *Note:* Trim the seams together diagonally across sharp corners, such as collar points and neck facing edges, before continuing to grade the seam.

## Notching and Clipping Seams

After grading, cut V-shaped notches from the seam allowance on outer curves. On inner curves, make small clips in the seam. Space the clips and notches around the edges so the curve will lie flat. Be careful not to clip through the stitching.

## Understitching Seams

Grade, clip, and notch the seams as needed. Work with the right side of the garment facing up. Turn the two seam allowances toward the under layer (facing, undercollar, etc.). Sew, using a regular machine stitch, through all layers about ⅛ inch (3 mm) from the seamline. Press the under-layer to the underside. Roll the seam slightly to the underside so it will not show on the finished garment.

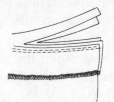

Trimming the seams at gradual widths.

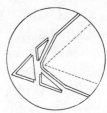

Trimming collar points diagonally.

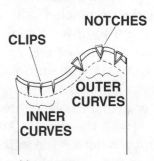

Clipping and notching a seam.

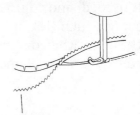

Understitching a facing.

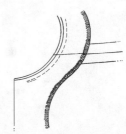

An understitched facing rolls smoothly to the inside of the garment and will not show from the right side of the garment.

## Handout 11

# GATHERING

Follow these steps for gathering:

1. Sew two evenly spaced rows of machine basting, using a long machine stitch. Leave a 2-inch (5 cm) length of thread at the beginning and end of each row. Stitch the first row on the seamline. Stitch the second row about ¼ inch (6 mm) from the seamline, inside the seam allowance. *Note:* If a large amount of fabric is to be gathered, divide the section to be gathered into four equal parts. Then stitch and gather each part separately.

2. To attach the gathered section: with right sides together, pin the center of the edge to be gathered to the center of the corresponding straight edge. Then pin the remaining sections of the edge to be gathered to the straight edge, matching all markings, notches, and seams.

3. Adjust gathers to fit the straight edge. First, secure one end of the basting stitches by wrapping the thread ends around a pin in a figure eight. Working from the other end, gently pull the loose ends of the bobbin threads. Slide the fabric along with your fingers. After gathering the amount you think is needed, secure threads by wrapping them around a pin. Measure the exact width needed, and adjust the gathers. Pin about every ½ inch (1.3 cm).

4. When stitching a gathered seam, sew with the gathered edge on top. Remove the pins as you sew.

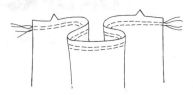

Step 1: Stitch two evenly-spaced rows of machine basting.

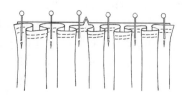

Step 2: Pin gathers evenly, matching all notches, markings, and seams.

Step 3: Secure the thread ends of gathers in a figure eight.

Step 3: Pull gathering threads, then adjust the gathers evenly.

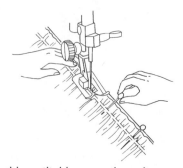

Step 4: Machine stitching a gathered seam.

## Handout 12

# PLEATS

Regardless of the type of pleat you're making, mark accurately and follow your guide sheet carefully for specific instructions. This general information will help you complete your pleats with speed and perfection.

1. Mark the fold lines and placement lines with thread markings. Use one color thread for the fold line and another color for the placement line. Take small stitches every 3 inches (7.5 cm) through the pattern tissue and fabric.
2. Clip the thread between the stitches. Remove the pattern tissue carefully to avoid pulling out your thread markings.
3. Baste each pleat in place along the entire fold line.
4. Press the pleats carefully, using a press cloth. Place strips of paper under the fold lines to prevent press mark ridges along the placement lines. For soft pleats, press lightly. For extra-sharp pleats, use a damp press cloth and allow the pleats to dry thoroughly before removing the garment from the ironing board. For a more permanent crease, you can have your pleats pressed professionally.
5. Complete your pleats according to the guide sheet instructions.

## Hemming Pleats

Reduce bulk at seams crossing the hem allowance by following these simple steps:
1. Clip the seam above the hem area.
2. Press the seam open below the clip.
3. Trim the seam allowances below the clip to reduce bulk.
4. Complete the hem.

Step 2: Clipping thread markings for pleats and removing the pattern tissue.

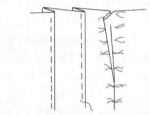

Step 3: Basting pleats in place.

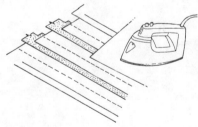

Step 4: When pressing pleats, use strips of brown paper under pleats to prevent press marks.

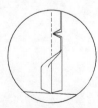

Steps 1 and 2: Before hemming pleats, clip the seam at the hemline and press the seam open below the clip.

Continued on next page

5. Fold the pleat, right sides together, with the seam on the edge of the fold.
6. Edgestitch the hem allowance of the pleat at the seam, through all thicknesses.

## Topstitching Pleats

Topstitching is not only a decorative finish but also a technique for holding pleats in place and helping them hang smoothly. It is normally done in the waist-to-hip area, through all thicknesses of fabric.

1. Mark each pleat with a pin to indicate where the topstitching will end.
2. With the garment right side up, topstitch through all thicknesses, starting at the pin and stitching to the top of the pleat.
3. Pull threads to the underside and tie.

## Edgestitching Pleats

Edgestitching is done along the fold of a pleat to give it a sharper crease. Always stitch from the bottom to the top after the hem is complete.

1. Press pleats carefully along the fold lines.
2. Edgestitch along the outside fold of the pleat from the bottom of the pleat to the top.

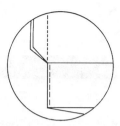

Step 6: Edgestitching the hem allowance of the pleat.

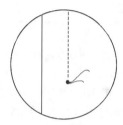

Step 3: Pull the topstitching threads to the underside of the pleat and tie them together.

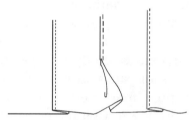

Step 2: Edgestitching pleats.

**Handout 13**

# POCKETS

Use the directions that follow to make square patch pockets, rounded patch pockets, or in-seam pockets.

## Square Patch Pockets

1. Finish the top edge of the pocket by turning the raw edge under ¼ inch (6 mm) to the wrong side; press; and stitch close to the edge. Another method is to simply serge the raw edge.
2. Turn the top pocket edge to the outside (right sides of fabric together) along the fold line to form the pocket facing. Pin.
3. Stitch along the seamline from the top of the pocket on one side to the top on the other side. Backstitch at both ends.
4. Trim the corners and seam allowance on the pocket facing to about ¼ inch (6 mm). Turn pocket facing right side out and press.
5. Fold the seam allowances under, along the stitching line. Press. This will give you a guide-line to work with in order to form a square corner.
6. To form a square corner, open the seam allow-ances. Fold the corners under diagonally to the stitching line and press. Trim the diagonal seam allowance to ¼ inch (6 mm). Refold the seam allowances on both sides of the corner to form a square edge. Press again.
7. Place the pocket on the outside of the gar-ment, with the wrong side down. Follow place-ment markings. Pin and baste.
8. Machine stitch close to the outer folded edge. Use the inside edge of the presser foot as a seam guide. Reinforce the top edge of the pocket by backstitching.

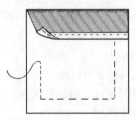
Step 3: Finish and face the pocket edge.

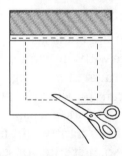
Step 4: Trim the pocket corners and seam allowance.

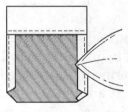
Step 6: Fold and press the pocket seam allowances.

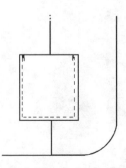
Step 8: Machine stitch the pocket in place.

Continued on next page

**TODAY'S TEEN CONSTRUCTION SKILLS** **31**

## Rounded Patch Pockets

For smooth, rounded curves without puckers and points, complete Steps 1 and 2 for square patch pockets, then continue as follows:

1. Stitch around the curve next to the seamline, in the seam allowance, using about 8 to 10 stitches per inch (each 2.5 cm).
2. Trim the seam allowance to about ¼ inch (6 mm) from the stitching line.
3. Pull up the stitches around the curves, just enough to draw in the seam allowance and shape the pocket curve.
4. Notch the seam allowance, if necessary, to reduce pressure and prevent puckers.
5. Press the pocket, forming smooth, evenly rounded curves.
6. Apply the pocket to the garment following Steps 7 and 8 for square patch pockets.

## In-Seam Pockets

Pockets that are enclosed in a seam may be cut in one piece with the garment section, especially if the garment fabric is lightweight. If the garment style calls for a heavier fabric, however, the pattern may include a separate pocket extension to be cut from lightweight lining fabric to reduce bulk. If so, first stitch or serge the pocket extensions to the garment sections. Then follow these steps for all in-seam pockets:

1. To prevent stretching along the pocket edge, reinforce the fold line with seam tape.
2. Mark the stitching line around the pocket.
3. Stitch the garment seams together, following the markings around the pocket area. Use shorter stitches near the corners to give them extra strength.

Step 1: Stitch around curved edges of pocket.

Step 2: Trim seam allowances.

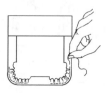

Step 3: Pull stitches around the curve to shape the pocket curve.

Step 4: Notch the seam allowance if necessary.

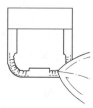

Step 5: Press rounded corners of the patch pocket.

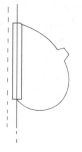

Sew in-seam pocket pieces to garment sections.

Step 1: Reinforce pocket fold line with seam tape.

Continued on next page

4. Clip the seam allowance on the back side of the garment at the top and bottom of the pocket. Clip to, but not through, the stitching.

5. Press the seams open, and press the pocket toward the garment front.

## Serged Seam Finish

To serge around the pocket edges, begin serging the seam at the garment hemline. Otherwise, it is very difficult to serge around the lower edge of the pocket without cutting into the garment. As you approach the lower edge of the pocket, pull the pocket forward to form a straightened line. Serge this edge, then guide the stitches around the pocket curve.

## Topstitching

For a decorative finish, you may topstitch the pocket on the garment front. Follow these steps for a smooth, even topstitching line:

1. Transfer the stitching line from the pattern tissue to a sheet of paper.

2. Cut the paper along the stitching line markings.

3. Smooth out the garment and pocket sections on a flat surface. Place the paper on the garment with the curved edge where the stitching line should be.

4. Topstitch the pocket to the garment front along the curved edge of the paper through all thicknesses.

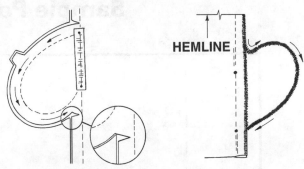

Step 4: Clip the seam allowance on the backside of garment.

Step 5: Press.

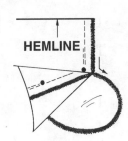

Straighten the seam while serging the pocket.

 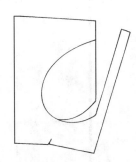

Step 1: Transfer the stitching line from the pattern.

Step 2: Cut paper along markings.

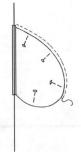

Step 4: Topstitch pocket edge to garment through all thicknesses.

Continued on next page

# Sample Pocket Pattern

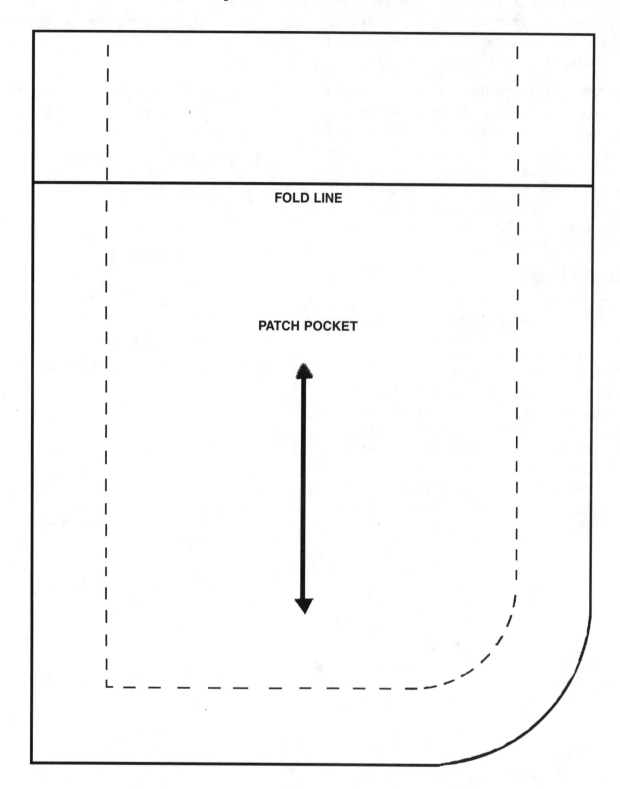

FOLD LINE

PATCH POCKET

### Handout 14

# COLLARS

Follow these basic steps for making all two-piece collars:

1. Pin the interfacing to the wrong side of the undercollar. Machine baste the interfacing to the undercollar ½ inch (1.3 cm) from the outer edge. If the collar is pointed, trim the corners off the interfacing before attaching it to the undercollar. If you are using fusible interfacing, trim off the interfacing ½ inch (1.3 cm) on all edges. Follow the manufacturer's directions for fusing.

2. With right sides together, pin the uppercollar and undercollar together.

3. Stitch the collar together on the seamline except at the neck edge. Use a short stitch length. Take one stitch diagonally across each corner of a pointed collar. This makes a neater point when the collar is turned.

4. Grade the seams. Trim the interfacing close to the stitching; trim the undercollar seam allowance to ¼ inch (6 mm); and trim the uppercollar seam allowance to ⅜ inch (1 cm). Trim both seam allowances diagonally across collar points about ⅛ inch (3 mm) from the stitching line. Clip the seam allowances on curves as needed for a smooth turn.

Step 1: Stitch sew-on interfacing to undercollar.

Step 1: Applying fusible interfacing to undercollar.

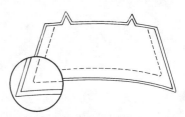

Step 3: Stitching collar pieces together. Take one diagonal stitch across the corner.

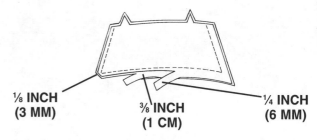

⅛ INCH (3 MM)      ⅜ INCH (1 CM)      ¼ INCH (6 MM)

Step 4: Grade the seam allowances on the collar.

⅛ INCH (3 MM)

Step 4: Trimming the collar point.

Continued on next page

5. On a pointed collar, understitch to within 1 inch (2.5 cm) from each point. On a round collar, understitch all around the seam.

6. Turn the collar right side out and gently push the points out. (Never use a scissors to do this. Use a point turner—a small tool you can buy at a fabric store.) Press the collar flat, being sure to roll the seam to the undercollar side so it will not show on the finished collar.

7. Baste the notched, raw neck edges together. Attach the collar to the garment as directed.

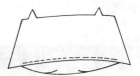

Step 5: Understitch seam allowances to undercollar.

Step 6: Use a point turner to gently push out the points of the collar.

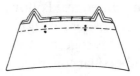

Step 7: Baste the neck edges of the collar together.

Continued on next page

# Sample Collar Pattern

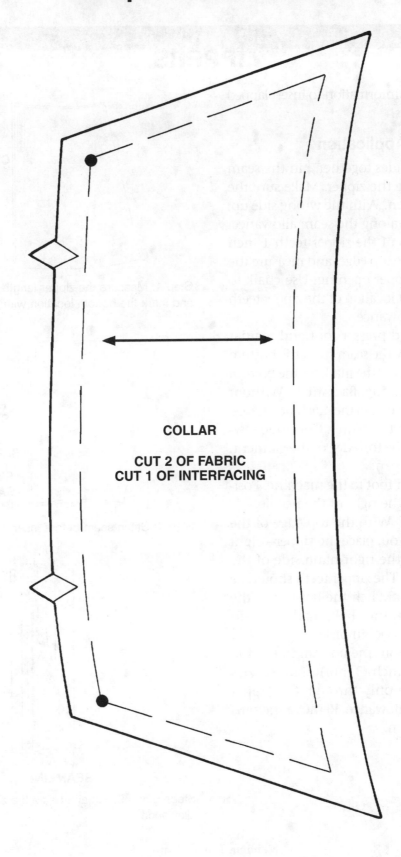

**COLLAR**

**CUT 2 OF FABRIC**
**CUT 1 OF INTERFACING**

## Handout 15

# ZIPPERS

Use the following information to insert lapped and centered zippers.

## Lapped Zipper Application

1. With the right sides together, pin the seam that will include the zipper. Make sure the top edges are even. With the wrong side up, place the zipper along the seam allowance. Position the top of the zipper teeth 1 inch (2.5 cm) from the top edge, and measure the length of the zipper opening. Use chalk to mark the bottom location of the zipper teeth on the seam allowance.

2. Using a standard presser foot and regular stitch length, sew the seam from the bottom of the garment up to the mark for the bottom of the zipper opening. Backstitch. Without removing the fabric from the machine, change the stitch length to basting. Continue sewing the seam to the top edge of the garment.

3. Press the seam open.

4. Attach the zipper foot to the machine. Position the foot to the right of the needle.

5. Open the zipper. With the top edge of the garment facing you, place the zipper—right side down—on the right-hand side of the seam allowance. The zipper teeth should be on the seamline. Match the bottom of the zipper teeth with the chalk mark made in Step 1. Pin the zipper in place.

6. Machine baste from the bottom to the top of the zipper, ⅛ inch (3 mm) from the zipper teeth. Stitch only through the zipper tape and seam allowance. Remove the pins as you reach them.

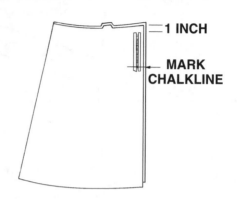

Step 1: Measure the zipper length against the garment and mark the bottom location with chalk.

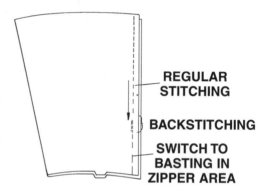

Step 2: Stitch seam before inserting the zipper.

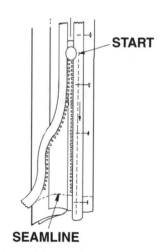

Steps 5 and 6: Pin and baste the zipper to the seam allowance.

Continued on next page

7. Close the zipper and turn it face up. Keep the garment to the left of the needle. Fold the seam allowance away from the zipper and pin in place. Move the zipper foot to the left side of the needle. Stitch through the folded edge of the seam allowance and the zipper tape from the bottom to the top of the zipper. This row of stitching should be close to the zipper teeth.

8. Fold the zipper over so the right side is flat against the other seam allowance. Turn the garment to the right. A tuck should form at the bottom of the zipper. Pin the zipper tape to the seam allowance only.

9. Machine baste the zipper to the seam allowance from the bottom to the top of the zipper. Stitch ⅛ inch (3 mm) from the zipper teeth.

10. Remove the garment from the machine and turn it right side out. Press lightly over the zipper area. Hand baste across the bottom of the zipper and up the side of the zipper, ⅜ inch (1 cm) from the seam.

11. Move the zipper foot to the right side of the needle, and begin stitching at the bottom of the zipper. Sew along the hand basting across the bottom of the zipper, stitching ½ inch (1.3 cm) out from the seam. To pivot the corner: stop with the needle in the fabric; lift the presser foot and turn the fabric so the top edge of the garment is facing you; lower the presser foot. Continue stitching along the basting, ½ inch (1.3 cm) from the seam, to the top of the garment. Backstitch ¼ inch (6 mm) at the top of the zipper to secure the stitching.

12. Pull the upper thread at the bottom of the zipper to the inside of the garment by using a hand sewing needle. Tie the upper and bobbin threads together and clip the threads close to the garment. Remove all basting stitches. Press.

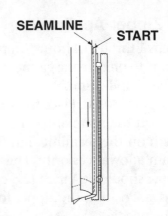

Step 7: Edgestitch through all layers close to the zipper teeth.

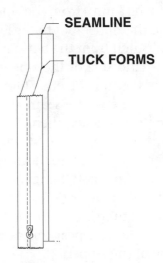

Step 9: Machine baste the zipper to the seam allowance.

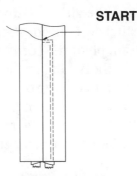

Step 11: On the right side, machine stitch the zipper in place along the hand basting.

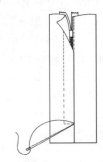

Step 12: Use a hand sewing needle to pull the upper thread at the bottom of the zipper to the inside and tie the threads together.

Continued on next page

## Centered Zipper Application

1. Repeat Steps 1 through 4 from "Lapped Zipper Application" to prepare the garment for "Centered Zipper Application."

2. Keep the zipper closed. Place the zipper right side down on the seam allowance with the zipper teeth on the seamline. Pin the zipper to the seam allowances only. The top teeth of the zipper should be 1 inch (2.5 cm) below the top edge. Position the zipper foot to the right of the needle.

3. Machine baste from the bottom to the top on the right-hand side of the zipper, stitching ⅛ inch (3 mm) from the zipper teeth. Reposition the zipper foot to the left side of the needle. Stitch from the bottom to the top of the left-hand side of the zipper, ⅛ inch (3 mm) from the zipper teeth. Stitch through the zipper tape and the seam allowance. Remove pins as you reach them.

4. Turn the garment right side up. Press lightly over the zipper area. Beginning at the center seam, hand baste along the bottom of the zipper and up one side ¼ inch (6 mm) from the seam. Stitch through the garment and the zipper tape. Repeat this step along the other side of the zipper.

5. With the zipper foot to the right of the needle, insert the machine needle on the seamline at the bottom of the zipper. Using the basting as a guide, stitch just outside the basting across the bottom, pivot the corner, and continue sewing along the basting up the right side of the zipper. Stitch to the top of the garment. Backstitch to secure stitching. Move the zipper foot to the left side of the needle. Repeat this process for the left side of the zipper.

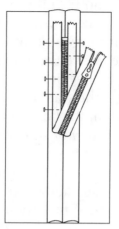

**PIN ZIPPER TO SEAM ALLOWANCE ONLY.**

Step 2: Close the zipper and place it right side down on the seam allowance with the zipper teeth on the seam line. Pin in place.

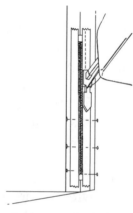

Step 3: Machine baste the zipper to the seam allowance, removing the pins while you sew.

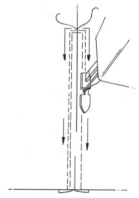

Step 5: Machine topstitch the zipper in place just outside the basting.

Continued on next page

**6.** Pull the upper threads at the bottom of the zipper to the inside of the garment, using a hand sewing needle. Tie the threads. Remove all basting stitches. Press.

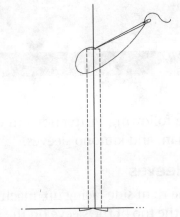

Step 6: Pull the threads at the bottom of the zipper to the inside of the garment and tie.

## Handout 16

# SLEEVES

Use the following instructions to complete set-in, raglan, and kimono sleeves.

## Set-In Sleeves

1. With the right side facing up, machine baste around the top of the sleeve on the seamline between the notches. Do not clip off the thread ends. Sew a second row of basting stitches ¼ inch (6 mm) from the first, inside the seam allowance.

2. To avoid making two sleeves to fit the same armhole, put both sleeves on a table with the right sides facing up. With right sides together, pin the underarm seam on each sleeve. Stitch the underarm seams. Finish the seam edges. Press the underarm seams open.

3. Match each sleeve to the garment with the right sides together. Pin each sleeve on the garment at the underarm seams, shoulder seams, notches, and markings. Insert pins on the seamline to hold the seam securely.

4. Pull the bobbin thread ends, starting at each notch, and ease the fabric toward the top until the sleeve fits the armhole. Secure threads around a pin in a figure eight. Distribute fullness evenly. Place pins ½ inch (1.3 cm) apart along the seamline. Keep the raw edges even. The sleeve should fit smoothly without puckers.

5. Machine stitch on the inside with the sleeve side facing up to be sure no puckers are caught in the seam. Begin and end the stitching at the underarm seam, backstitching to secure the seam. Then make a second row of stitching between the notches in the underarm area. Sew ⅛ inch (3 mm) from the first row of stitching, inside the seam allowance.

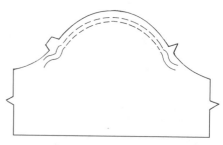

Step 1: Machine baste around the top of the sleeve between the notches.

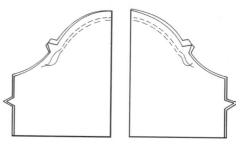

Step 2: Stitch the underarm sleeve seam.

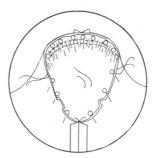

Step 3: Pin each sleeve to the garment with right sides together.

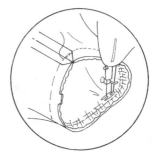

Step 5: Machine stitch the sleeves in place with the sleeve side up.

Continued on next page

6. Trim the seam between the notches at the underarm to ¼ inch (6 mm). Zigzag or serge the seam allowances together to finish the seam. Press the armhole seam toward the sleeve. Repeat this process for the remaining sleeve.

## Raglan Sleeves

1. Stitch the shoulder dart or seam. Cut the dart open along the fold line to 1 inch (2.5 cm) from the point and press open.
2. Pin the diagonal seams of the sleeve to the garment front and back with the right sides together. Make sure you match notches, markings, and the underarm edges.
3. Stitch seams on the seamline. Sew a second row of stitching ¼ inch (6 mm) from the seamline in the seam allowance. Stitch from the underarm edge up to the notches.
4. Clip to the first row of stitching at the notches. Trim the underarm close to the inside row of stitching. Press the seams open between the notches and the neckline.
5. Stitch the underarm seam of the sleeve and side seam. Press open.

## Kimono Sleeves

1. With right sides together, pin the shoulder seam. Stitch on the seamline, backstitching at both ends of the seam. Press the seam open.
2. With right sides together, pin the underarm seam. Stitch the underarm seam on the seamline. Stitch again at the underarm curve, ¼ inch (6 mm) from the seamline.
3. Clip the underarm curve of the seam. Press the seam open, except at the underarm curve.

Step 6: Trim the underarm seam between the notches.

Step 1: Stitch the shoulder dart or seam.

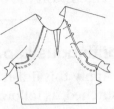

Step 3: Stitch the sleeve seams to the garment.

Step 4: Clip and trim the underarm seam allowance close to the inside row of stitching.

Step 5: Sew the underarm seam and side seam.

Step 1: Sew the shoulder seams and press open.

Step 2: Stitch the underarm seam, reinforcing the underarm with double stitching.

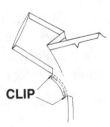

CLIP

Step 3: Clip the seam and press as directed.

**Handout 17**

# CUFFS

A standard cuff is made from a separate piece of fabric attached to the bottom edge of a sleeve. The sleeve has an opening, or placket, that corresponds to the cuff opening. The method used most often to finish the opening is the continuous lap, a strip of fabric that binds the opening edges.

## Continuous Lap Opening

Apply this finish before the underarm seam is stitched, as follows:

1. Using your pattern tissue as a guide, mark the slash and stitching lines for the sleeve opening.
2. Reinforce the opening on the stitching line with small stitches, about 20 per inch (for every 25 mm).
3. Slash the fabric between the reinforcement stitching, cutting up to, but not through, the stitches.
4. Spread the edges of the opening apart so they almost form a straight line.
5. Cut a piece of fabric for the binding 1¼ inches (32 mm) wide and twice the length of the slash marking on the pattern guide sheet. Use either the true bias or the straight grain of the fabric for the continuous lap.
6. With right sides together, pin the fabric strip to the slashed edge so the stitching line of the opening is ¼ inch (6 mm) from the edge of the strip. The extra fabric at the point of the opening will form a tuck.
7. Working with the sleeve side up, stitch along the reinforcement stitches. As you come to the point of the opening, keep the tucked sleeve fabric out of the way. Continue stitching.
8. Press the seam allowances toward the continuous lap. Press under ¼ inch (6 mm) on the remaining long edge of the strip.

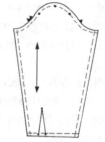
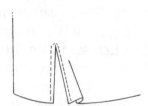

Step 1: Transfer slash line markings from the pattern to the fabric.

Step 3: Reinforce the opening and then slash the fabric between the reinforcement stitching.

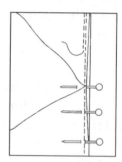

Steps 6 and 7: Pin and stitch the continuous lap to the sleeve.

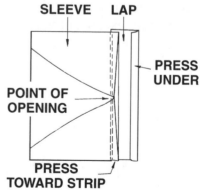

Step 8: Press the seam allowances toward the continuous lap.

Continued on next page

9. Pin this edge over the seam on the inside of the sleeve and slipstitch in place.

## Sewing the Cuffs

Once the sleeve opening is finished, stitch the underarm seam of the sleeve. Then follow these steps to make and attach the cuffs:

1. Interface each cuff following your guide sheet and the instructions given for interfacing.
2. Press the long unnotched seam allowance of the cuff to the wrong side of the fabric along the seamline and baste if necessary.
3. Trim the turned-under seam allowance to ¼ inch (6 mm) from the seamline.
4. Pin the notched edge of the cuff to the sleeve, right sides together, matching markings. Stitch.
5. Grade the seam allowances. Press the seam allowances toward the cuff.
6. Fold the cuff on the fold line, right sides together. Stitch the ends of the cuff.
7. Grade the seam allowances of the end seams and trim the corners diagonally.
8. Fold the cuff to the wrong side of the sleeve, matching the seamline of the trimmed edge to the seam that joins the cuff to the sleeve. Slipstitch along the seamline from the inside of the sleeve.

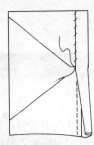

Step 9: Pin the remaining edge over seam and slip-stitch in place.

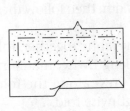

Steps 1 and 2: Interface the cuff and press under the unnotched edge of cuff as instructed.

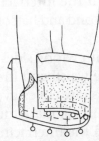

Step 4: Stitch notched edge of cuff to sleeve.

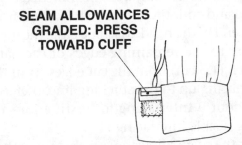

SEAM ALLOWANCES GRADED: PRESS TOWARD CUFF

Step 5: Grade the seam allowances and press them toward the cuff.

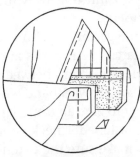

Step 7: Grade end seams and trim corners.

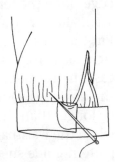

Step 8: Fold the cuff to the wrong side of sleeve and slipstitch along the seamline.

**Handout 18**

# WAISTBANDS

Use the following directions to complete attached, elastic, and drawstring waistbands.

## Attached Waistbands

Cut the interfacing the same length as the waistband and half of its width, then follow these steps:

1. With wrong sides of the fabric together, fold the waistband in half lengthwise, matching the raw edges evenly. Press along the fold. This will mark the lengthwise fold.

2. Pin the interfacing to the wrong side of the waistband, along the notched edge. The inside edge of the interfacing will be on the lengthwise fold.

3. Machine baste the interfacing to the waistband ½ inch (1.3 cm) from the notched edge. Begin and end stitching ½ inch (1.3 cm) from each end of the band. Machine baste the interfacing to the remaining edges of the band ½ inch (1.3 cm) from the cut edges. Trim the interfacing up to the stitching line. (Refer to Handout 9 Interfacing for instructions on using fusible interfacing.)

4. Press the seam allowance on the unnotched edge to the wrong side along the seamline. As an alternative, you can serge the unnotched edge along the seamline, trimming away the seam allowance as you serge.

5. Pin the waistband to the garment, with the right sides together. Match the notches and ease the garment to the waistband between the markings. One end of the waistband will be longer than the other to give an underlap when the waistband is fastened. Check your pattern guide sheet to make sure the extension is on the correct side of the opening.

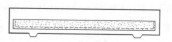
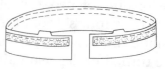

Step 3: Machine baste the interfacing to the notched edge of the waistband.

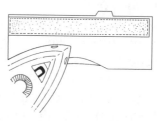

Step 4: Press the unnotched side of the waistband under, along the seamline.

Step 4: You can also serge the unnotched edge of the waistband.

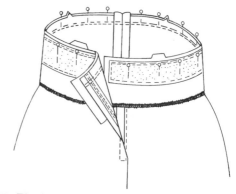

Step 5: Pin the waistband to the garment.

Continued on next page

6. Stitch on the seamline from one end of the waistband to the other. Backstitch at both ends. Grade the seam. Trim the waistband seam allowance to ¼ inch (6 mm) and the garment seam allowance to ⅜ inch (1 cm). Press the seam flat and then up toward the waistband.

7. Fold the waistband in half lengthwise with right sides together. Pin and stitch the seam at each end of the waistband. The stitching will be even with the folded edge of the zipper on the overlap. The underlap will be longer. Trim the seams to ¼ inch (6 mm). Trim the corners diagonally, being careful not to cut the stitching.

8. Turn the waistband right side out. Check to be sure the corners are square. Press along the fold line.

9. Pin the unnotched side of the waistband to the seam allowance on the inside of the garment. Slipstitch the turned (or serged) edge to the waistline seam.

## Elastic Waistbands

The following directions are for making a casing that is 1 inch (2.5 cm) wide, which will enclose ¾-inch-wide (2 cm) elastic.

1. Serge or use a zigzag stitch around the top edge of the garment if the raw edges need to be finished.

2. Fold the waistline edge of the garment over 1¼ inches (3.2 cm), matching the wrong sides together to form a casing. Press the folded edge.

3. Stitch a seam 1 inch (2.5 cm) from the folded edge of the casing. Begin stitching at the center, back, or side seam. Leave a 1½-inch (3.8 cm) opening to insert elastic. Backstitch at each end of the seam.

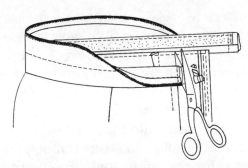

Step 6: Trim the seams at the ends of the waistband. Trim the corners diagonally.

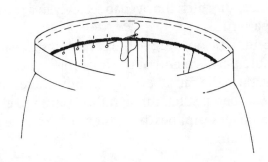

Step 9: Slipstitch the turned or serged edge to the waistline seam.

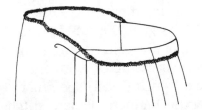

Step 2: After finishing the edge, fold over the waistline edge of the garment to form a casing.

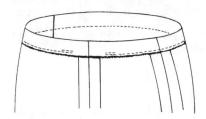

Step 3: Stitch a seam 1 inch (2.5 cm) from the folded edge of casing.

Continued on next page

4. Cut a piece of elastic to fit snugly around your waist. Remember, it must be able to slide over your hips. Add 2 inches (5 cm) to allow you to overlap and stitch the elastic together.

5. Put a safety pin through one end of the elastic. After securely closing the pin, insert the pin and elastic into the opening in the casing. Pull the pin and elastic through the casing, using the pin to guide the elastic. Hold onto the loose end of the elastic.

6. Overlap the elastic ends 1 inch (2.5 cm). Machine stitch the overlap securely in a square pattern.

7. Stitch the opening of the casing closed. Backstitch at each end of the opening.

8. Adjust the fabric evenly around the elastic waistband. Stitch through the casing and elastic at all seamlines, backstitching to secure all stitching.

## Drawstring Waistbands

Here are guidelines for a drawstring casing that has an opening in a seam:

1. At the seam where the drawstring is to be pulled through to the outside, stitch 1¼ inches (3.2 cm) of the seam starting at the top of the garment. Backstitch at both ends.

2. Leave a ¾-inch (2 cm) opening in the seam below the 1¼-inch (3.2 cm) stitched seam. Complete the seam below the ¾-inch (2 cm) opening. Backstitch at both ends of the seam.

3. Fold ¼ inch (6 mm) of the top edge of the garment to the inside. Press. (You may also serge the top edge, trimming off ¼ inch [6 mm] as you serge.)

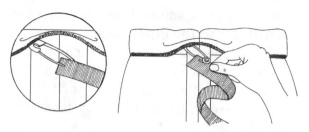

Step 5: Insert a safety pin and elastic into the casing.

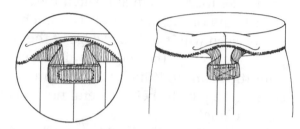

Step 6: Overlap and stitch the elastic ends together.

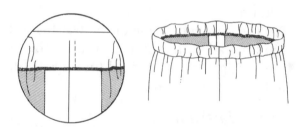

Step 8: Stitch the casing closed and stitch through the elastic and casing at the seamlines.

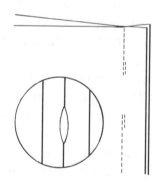

Step 2: Stitch the seam, leaving an opening for the drawstring in the seam.

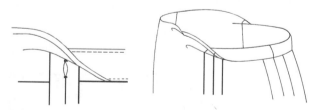

Step 3: Finish the top edge and fold the waistline edge over to form a casing.

Continued on next page

4. Fold the top edge of the garment over 1 inch (2.5 cm) to the inside, forming a casing. Press along the fold line. Stitch close to the lower edge of the casing. Backstitch at the beginning and end of the stitching.

5. Put a safety pin in one end of the drawstring. On the outside, insert the pinned drawstring through the casing opening and pull the drawstring through the casing and then back out of the opening. (Be sure to hold on to the loose end of the drawstring so it will not be pulled through.) Tie a knot in each end of the drawstring. Distribute the fullness evenly.

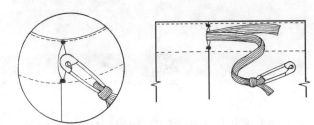

Step 5: Insert the safety pin and drawstring into casing.

## Handout 19

# HEMS

Use the following directions to prepare and finish hems.

## Preparing the Hem

1. Put on shoes with the heel height you expect to wear with the finished garment. Then decide on the most attractive length for the garment.
2. Have another person measure the correct length up from the floor using a measuring stick, and place pins or chalk marks at the same distance all the way around the garment. Check to be sure the markings form an even line. Make any changes needed. (For pants, simply turn up an even distance all the way around and check that the length is right with your heel height.)
3. Using the marked line as a guide, turn the hem to the wrong side of the garment. Pin along the fold line. Place pins at right angles to the folded edge.
4. Measure the hem width needed plus ¼ inch (6 mm) for finishing. Use a sewing gauge, cardboard notched at the correct hem width or a ruler, to mark the correct hem width. Cut off any extra fabric from the edge of the hem or serge on the marked line, cutting off the extra fabric and finishing the raw edge at the same time.
5. Machine stitch ¼ inch (6 mm) from the cut edge. Stitch only through the hem, not the outside of the garment.
6. If necessary, ease in extra fullness at the hemline so the hem will not be bulky and lumpy. Shrink the fullness along the hem by steam pressing in the direction of the grain. For fabrics that do not shrink, ease out the fullness by pulling up on the bobbin thread at different points along the stitching to take out the fullness. Press with steam to flatten the eased fabric.

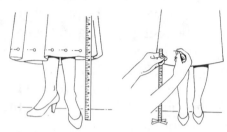

Step 2: Measure the skirt hem up from the floor.

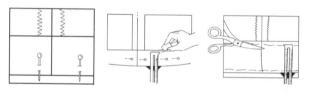

Step 2: Check the pinned pant hem with the heel height.

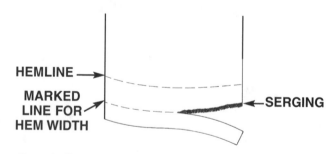

Steps 3 and 4: Pin up the hem on the marked line. Measure and mark the finished hem allowance width using a hem gauge and chalk.

HEMLINE ——→

MARKED LINE FOR HEM WIDTH →

←—SERGING

Step 4: Cut or serge off the hem edge.

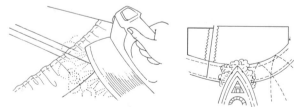

Step 6: Press up the hem in the direction of the grain.

Continued on next page

## Finishing the Hem Edge

Unless you serged the hem edge above, the raw edge must be finished to prevent raveling. Follow one of these methods:

- **Turned and stitched.** Fold the edge under ¼ inch (6 mm) and press. Edgestitch along the fold.
- **Seam tape.** Pin tape or lace to the outside of the raw edge. Be sure ¼ inch (6 mm) of the seam tape overlaps the edge of the fabric. Machine stitch the tape to the hem allowance only.

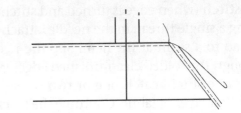
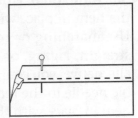

Turned and stitched hem finish.

## Pressing the Hem

Turn the hem allowance to the inside along the marked line. Press the hem in place from the wrong side only. Press along the hem line only so the top edge of the hem allowance won't form a ridge on the right side. If necessary, put strips of brown paper between the hem allowance and the garment.

Taped hem finish.

## Stitching the Hem

Here are several methods that you can use to stitch the hem of a garment:

- **Whipstitch** (when hem is finished with seam tape or by serging). Using a single strand of thread in a needle, attach the thread to the hem at a seam. Take small, even stitches by catching both the garment and the edge of the seam tape, lace, or serging in each stitch. Pick up only one or two threads of fabric as you sew.

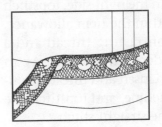

**BROWN PAPER**

Pressing the hem.

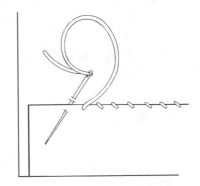

Whipstitched hem.

Continued on next page

- **Slipstitch** (when edge is turned and stitched). Using a single thread in the needle, attach the thread to a seam at the hem. Slip the needle through the folded clean-finished edge. With the same stitch, catch one or two threads in the other layer of fabric. Continue the stitches, always slipping the needle through the fold and then into the outer layer of fabric
- **Machine stitch.** From the right side, topstitch the hem in place within the hem allowance. Use matching or contrasting thread and a straight, zigzag, or decorative stitch. As an alternative, you could insert and thread a double needle in the machine, and topstitch the hem in place with the straight stitch.

Slipstitched hem.

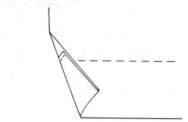

Machine stitched hem.

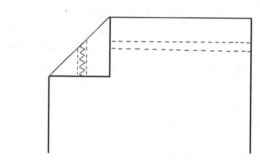

Double needle machine stitched hem.

## Handout 20

## FASTENERS

Use the directions that follow for hooks and eyes, snaps, and buttons. Remember that fasteners are the finishing touches on your garments.

### Hooks and Eyes

Two different methods are generally used for applying hooks and eyes. The directions that follow show you how to apply hooks and eyes for edges that overlap and for edges that meet.

### Edges That Overlap

1. Place the hook on the underside of the overlap, at least ⅛ inch (3 mm) from the edge. Using small stitches and a single thread in the needle, stitch around each loop or ring. Sew through one layer of fabric so that the stitches will not show on the right side.
2. Bring the needle between the two thicknesses of fabric to the end of the hook. Take 3 to 4 stitches around the end of the hook so it is held down firmly.
3. Overlap the edge and mark the position of the straight eye on the left-hand side with a pin.
4. Stitch the eye in place around both loops, using small stitches. Fasten the thread securely and clip.

### Edges That Meet

1. Sew the hook ⅛ inch (3 mm) in from the edge. Stitch around each loop and the end of the hook, using a single thread in the needle and small stitches. Sew through one layer of fabric so that the stitches will not show on the right side.
2. Match the garment edges. Position the round eye so that the loop extends ⅛ inch (3 mm) beyond the edge. (When the hook and eye are attached, the garment edges should meet exactly.) Stitch the eye in place using small stitches. Secure the thread, and clip close to the fabric.

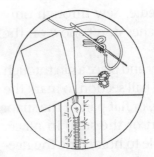

Step 1: Place and stitch the hook to the underside of the overlap.

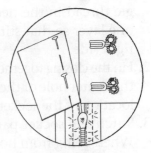

Step 3: Overlap the edge and mark the position of the straight eye.

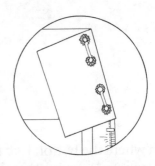

Step 4: Stitch the straight eye in place.

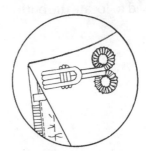

Step 1: For edges that meet, sew hook ⅛ inch (3 mm) from the edge.

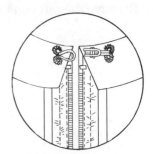

Step 2: Match garment edges and place the round eye so it extends ⅛ inch (3 mm) beyond the edge.

Continued on next page

## Snaps

Here are some guidelines for applying snaps:

1. Place the ball section of the snap on the underside of the overlap, about ⅛ inch (3 mm) from the edge. Make several small stitches close together in each hole of the snap using a single thread in the needle. Sew through only one layer so that stitches don't show on the right side.

2. Pin the closing together and place a pin through the center hole of the ball section to mark the location of the socket, or flat part of the snap.

3. Stitch the socket part of the snap in place. When going from hole to hole, slide the needle through one hole and under the snap to the next hole. Fasten the thread when finished.

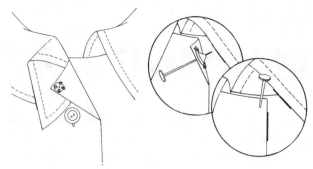

Step 1: Place the ball section of the snap ⅛ inch (3 mm) from the edge of overlap.

Step 2: Pin through the ball section to mark the placement of the socket section of snap.

Step 3: Finished snap placement.

## Buttons

1. Place a pin where the button is to be located. Select a matching thread color.

2. Double the thread in the needle and knot both ends together. Bring the needle up from the wrong side to the right side of the garment.

3. Take a small stitch to secure the thread knot.

4. Remove the pin you used to locate the button.

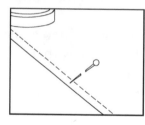

Step 1

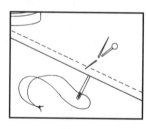

Step 2

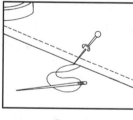

Step 3

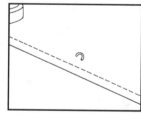

Step 4

Continued on next page

5. Bring the needle through the button. If the button doesn't have a shank, place a toothpick across the top of the button to allow for a thread shank.
6. Make several stitches through the fabric and the button, over the toothpick, and back down through the button and the fabric.
7. Remove the toothpick. Bring the needle and thread between the button and the fabric. Wrap the thread around the threads under the button several times to make a thread shank.
8. Bring the needle back to the wrong side of the fabric and fasten the thread securely to the fabric. Clip the thread.

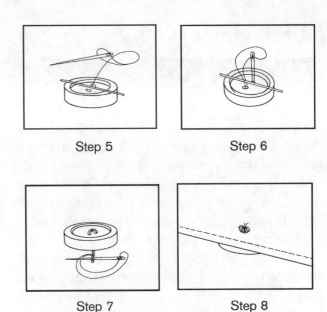

Step 5          Step 6

Step 7          Step 8

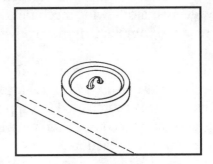

Finished button.

## Handout 21

# WHAT IS A SERGER?

A serger, sometimes called an overlock sewing machine, is a special type of sewing machine that can trim, stitch, and finish a seam in one step. It is a time-saving machine that gives a more finished, professional look to your sewn garments and operates at nearly twice the speed of a conventional sewing machine.

Sergers first became available to home sewers in Japan in 1967, when one company adapted them from the clothing production industry and introduced them to dressmakers, tailors, and drapery-makers. Their popularity soon spread, and now every major sewing machine company offers a serger to complement their conventional machine.

A serger cannot replace your regular sewing machine, but must be used with it. Buttonholes and a regular straight stitch used for zippers, topstitching, and garment construction must be done with a conventional machine.

## Sewing Serger Seams

A serger does not have a bobbin and top thread like a conventional sewing machine. Instead, it forms an overlock stitch using loopers. The loopers do not pass through the fabric as the stitch is formed; they go over the edge, so they can be threaded with heavy or decorative threads. Because of the way the stitch is formed, a serger must always sew over the edge it is encasing.

Different kinds of seams can be made on sergers, depending on the number of threads used and the number of needle options on a particular model. All sergers have cutting knives, use more than one spool of thread, and have a tension dial for each thread spool. Some have two needles. The most common kinds of sergers use either three or four cones of thread at one time. More information on seaming can be found in H0-23 Serger Threads.

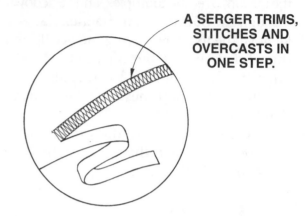

A trimmed and stitched serger seam.

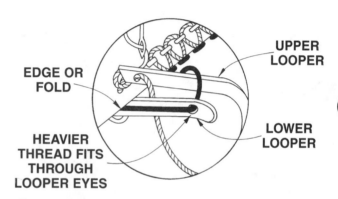

Serger stitches are formed over the edge of the fabric.

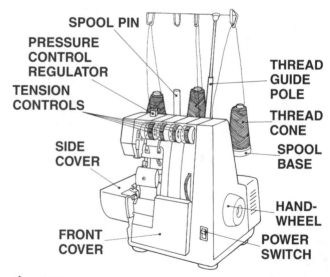

A serger.

Continued on next page

Some sergers have a feature called "differential feed," meaning there are two sets of feed dogs (the teeth that move fabric through the machine) that can operate at different speeds. Using the differential feed prevents the creation of wavy, stretched-out seams on very stretchable knits. It can also be used to gather one layer of fabric to another to create a ruffle and to keep lightweight, silky fabrics from puckering.

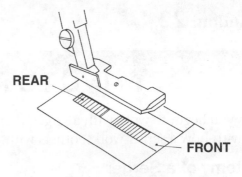
Differential feed.

## What Can a Serger Do?

A serger can duplicate many techniques found in ready-made clothing and can sew on almost any fabric. Some kinds of things sergers do best are:

- **Rolled edges.** On everything from napkins and placemats to the sheerest chiffon fabrics, the serger can produce a firm, attractive edge finish on only one layer of fabric.
- **Ravel-free seam finishes.** The serger can finish the edges of a straight-stitched seam or can actually sew a seam itself.
- **Stretchable seams.** Serged seams on active wear, swimsuits, and other knits have built-in stretch to keep them from breaking.
- **Decorative seaming.** Decorative seaming is a serger specialty—any kind of thread or yarn that will fit through the looper eyes can be used. Later in this booklet, we will learn about techniques called flatlocking and rolled hemming.

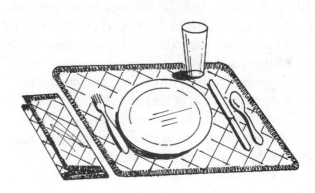
Rolled edge.

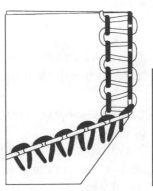
Ravel-free seam finish.

Stretchable seams.

Decorative seams.

# GETTING TO KNOW YOUR SERGER

As you begin to work with a serger, there are several new words and sewing terms to learn. Some deal with how a serger works, others with the parts of the serger.

## Anatomy of a Serger

Each model and brand of serger differs in outside appearance, but the basic parts are similar. These are shown in the illustration on the right side of this page. The look will vary with the number of thread spools and needles used to create a particular stitch, so the illustration shows the most common kind of serger, a ¾-thread model.

Serger models are often referred to with numbers detailing the number of threads used to form a stitch. For example, you will see models referred to as 2-thread, 3/4-thread (meaning it can sew either a 3-thread or 4-thread stitch), 5-thread, and 2/3/4-thread (meaning it can sew a 2-thread, a 3-thread, or a 4-thread stitch).

## Serger Vocabulary

1. **Balanced stitch:** A stitch used for seam sewing where the looper threads interlock at the fabric edge.
2. **Chaining off:** Serging off the edge of fabric to complete a seam or edge finish.
3. **Chain stitch:** A stitch available on 4/2- and 5-thread sergers that does not overcast the edge. A chain stitch is like the closing on most pet food bags—it looks like a straight stitch, but can pull out readily. Also called a safety stitch.
4. **Differential feed:** A feature available on some models of sergers to help produce a flat, distortion-free seam on stretchable knits and to help gather or ease other fabrics.
5. **Feed dogs:** The grooved teeth in front of and under the presser foot that feed the fabric into the serger.
6. **Flatlocking:** A decorative stitch often done with novelty threads. One side of the stitch has a ladder look and the other side has a looped look.

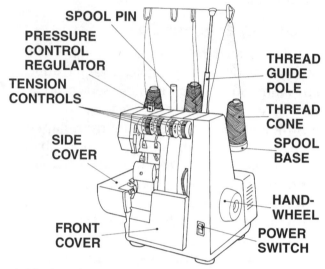

A 3/4-thread serger and its parts.

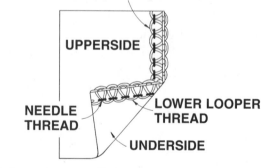

A balanced serger stitch.

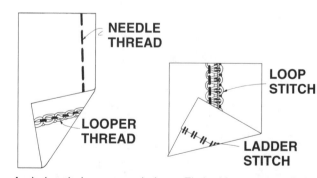

A chain stitch serger stitch.    Flatlocking serger stitch.

Continued on next page

7. **Knives:** The blades that trim fabric as it's being serged. Most models have knives that are retractable, for serging over a folded edge without risk of cutting the fabric.

8. **Loopers:** Arms that carry thread to form the overlock stitch. Serger stitches are formed with an upper and a lower looper.

9. **Overcast:** The portion of the serger stitch encasing the fabric edges.

10. **Overlock:** Another name for the serger or the portion of the serger stitch encasing the fabric edges.

11. **Rolled hem or rolled edge:** A narrow, compact stitch that rolls under the edge of the fabric.

12. **Seam sealant:** A liquid used to secure threads at the end of a line of stitching so they don't have to be knotted.

13. **Stitch finger:** The projecting metal prong over which stitches are formed. The completed stitch and fabric slide off the back of the stitch finger.

14. **Stitch length:** The distance (in millimeters) between the points where the needle enters the fabric to form stitches.

15. **Stitch width:** The distance from the needle to the trimmed edge of the fabric after a stitch is formed.

16. **Tension control:** The dial or knob with inner disks that apply pressure to the thread as it passes through the disks. There is one tension control for each spool of thread used in forming the serger stitch.

17. **Thread chain:** Stitches formed without fabric.

18. **Tying on:** A method of changing thread on the serger without unthreading it completely. Threads are cut above the tension controls and a new color tied on and pulled through the threading pattern.

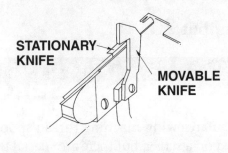

Serger knives.

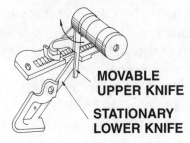

Serger knives.

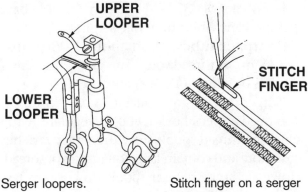

Serger loopers.          Stitch finger on a serger throat plate.

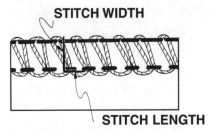

Stitch length and stitch width.

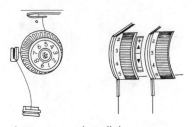

Two types of serger tension dials.

**Handout 23**

# SERGER THREADS

Regular sewing machine thread spools can be used on a serger, but there are special threads designed especially for sergers. Serger thread is "cross-wound" for smoother feeding, as compared to the "parallel-wound" varieties used on a regular sewing machine.

Serger thread can be found on three different kinds of spool types:

- **Cones:** Hold up to 6,000 yards (5,490 m) of thread. Because cones often vibrate during high-speed serging, most machines come with plastic cone inserts to hold them in place.
- **King tubes:** Hold less thread (usually about 1,500 yards [1,373 m] and have a wide base to prevent vibration while serging.
- **Compact tubes:** Hold about 1,000 yards (915 m) of thread, but store easier than king tubes because of their shape.

Serger threads are available in basic colors. If you need a special color, choose regular sewing machine thread spools since the serger varieties cost more and contain larger quantities of thread. However, since regular spools do contain less thread than the serger varieties, you must watch closely to be sure you don't run out of thread!

If you use regular thread spools on the serger, insert a spool cap, which generally comes with the machine, to keep the thread from catching in the end notch and breaking your stitches. Always place the spool with the notch down.

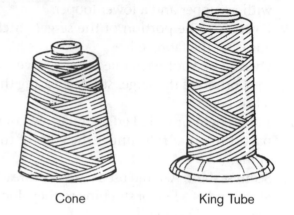

Cone           King Tube

Compact Tube

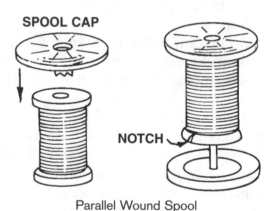

**SPOOL CAP**

**NOTCH**

Parallel Wound Spool

Continued on next page

## Specialty Threads

Because only the needle thread penetrates the fabric when serging, many novelty threads are appropriate for decorative serging that will be visible on the finished garment. Specialty threads are generally used only in the serger loopers and are combined with regular serger thread in the needle.

Look for these decorative threads to experiment with:

- **Rayon:** Shiny thread available in a wide range of sizes; comes in solid colors and variegated blends.
- **Topstitching:** Heavier thread with a flat finish.
- **Texturized nylon:** Crimped and twisted thread used for rolled hemming to give a soft, but completely covered edge.
- **Pearl cotton/crochet cotton:** Twisted thread with a sheen; used to create a braided-look edging.
- **Metallic:** Shiny thread that creates a glittering edge for special occasion garments.
- **Ribbon:** Very narrow strands used to create a crocheted-look edging.
- **Yarn:** Two-ply strands that produce a braid-like effect.

## Tension Adjustments

Always test-serge scraps of your fabric before beginning your project to allow for tension adjustments, especially when using decorative threads and when using different weights of threads in the loopers than in the needle(s).

As a general rule, the heavier the thread, the looser the tension and the lighter the thread, the tighter the tension. Remember, with the serger you can adjust the tension separately for each looper and each needle.

Experimentation is fun, but be patient until you get the look you want.

## Handout 24

# SERGER TENSION

Setting the proper tension is perhaps the most feared aspect of serging. (The term tension simply means the amount of tightness or looseness of a particular thread.) On a conventional sewing machine, there are bobbin and needle tension controls, and you adjust them only if the stitching doesn't look correct. On a serger, you can adjust the tension on each spool of thread—one or two needle threads and one or two looper threads. Tension is adjusted not only when the stitch does not look correct, but also when you change fabric, thread type, stitch width, or stitch length. In addition, if you use one type of thread in the needle and another type in the loopers, tension will need to be adjusted. It's a good idea to understand tension before using a serger.

Serger brands vary in the kind of tension controls they offer. Some have knobs on the machine front; others have dials recessed into the machine front. Most controls are numbered from 0 to 9: a few brands offer plus (+) symbol and minus (–) symbol indicators. No matter what they look like, all tension controls function the same way —they have disks inside that clamp down against the threads to create tension.

On numbered tension dials, a higher number indicates more tension on the thread, and a lower number indicates less tension. On dials with a plus (+) or minus (–), a plus (+) indicates more tension and a minus (–) less tension.

Always test-serge a sample of your garment fabric before sewing on the actual project to check tensions.

## Balanced Tension

For normal serger sewing, the stitch should appear "balanced." This means the upper and lower looper threads hug the top and bottom of the seam and meet exactly at the edge. The needle thread looks like a line of straight stitching on the top of the fabric and appears only as tiny loops on the underside.

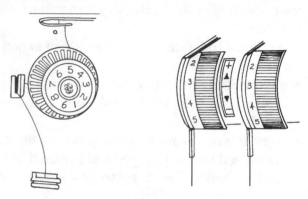

Serger tension controls.

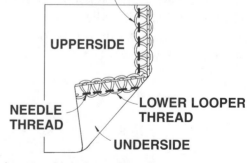

UPPER LOOPER THREAD

UPPERSIDE

NEEDLE THREAD

LOWER LOOPER THREAD

UNDERSIDE

Serged seam with balanced tension.

Continued on next page

## Needle Thread Tension

The needle tension needs adjusting only if the seam does not look correct. If the needle thread tension is too loose, the seam will spread apart if it's pulled gently. If the needle thread tension is too tight, the seam will pucker and not lie flat.

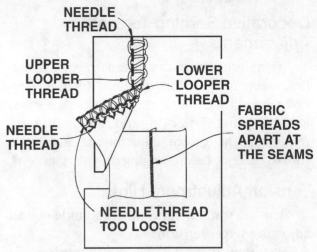

Needle thread is too loose. Loops form on underside.

## Upper Looper Tension

The upper looper tension controls the top thread of the serger stitch. If it's too tight, the lower looper thread will be pulled to the top of the stitching. If it's too loose, the thread will overhang the fabric edge or be pulled to the underside.

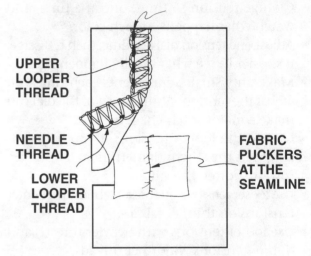

Needle thread is too tight. Fabric puckers at the needle line.

## Lower Looper Tension

The lower looper tension controls the bottom thread of the serger stitch. If it's too tight, the upper looper thread will be pulled to the underside. If it's too loose, the thread will hang off the fabric edge or be pulled to the topside.

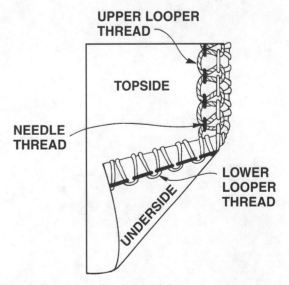

Upper looper tension is too tight.

Continued on next page

## Decorative Serging Tension Adjustments

When using decorative threads (rayons, metallics, yarns, narrow ribbons, etc.), it will be necessary to adjust the tensions to achieve the stitch look you want. Flatlocking and rolled hemming require special tension adjustments. Always be sure to practice before serging on your garment.

## Tension Adjustment Hints

Here are some helpful hints to guide you in adjusting serger tension:

- For starters, to get a better look at tension, use a different color thread on each serger spool. Change tension settings, one at a time, and watch what happens to each color.
- Adjust one tension dial at a time, then test-serge; it's easier to see what's really happening.
- Make only small adjustments each time you adjust the tension. A small turn of the dial can make a major stitch change.
- Loosen the looper tensions if you widen or lengthen the stitch; tighten them if you narrow or shorten the stitch.
- Use looser tensions on thicker fabrics and tighter tensions on thinner fabrics.
- Use looser tensions with heavier threads and tighter tensions with finer threads.

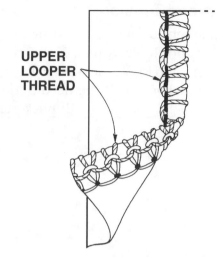

Upper looper tension is too loose.

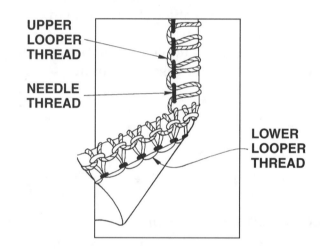

Lower looper tension is too tight.

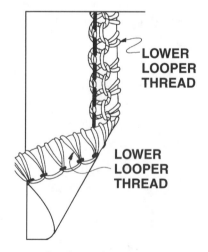

Lower looper tension is too loose.

## Handout 25

# SERGER SEAMS

The serger can be used to stitch a seam or to create an edge finish for a conventionally-stitched seam. A serger can trim, seam, and finish in one quick operation and can also produce a flexible seam for knitwear and stretch fabrics. Once a seam is serged, however, there are no seam allowances remaining. If a size increase is needed, alterations should be done prior to serging!

### Serged Seams

When serger seaming, it is important to guide the fabric straight into the knives because they cut the fabric before the stitch is formed.

A 3-thread serger will produce a seam with greater flexibility than the 4- or 5-thread models. The more threads involved in the stitch making, the more durable the seam. The illustration at the right shows various kinds of serger seams, depending on the brand, number of threads, and needles. Not all sergers can do every stitch.

To begin any serger seam, leave a 4-inch (10 cm) thread tail. Place the fabric right sides together and put the seamline in front of the presser foot. On most sergers it isn't necessary to lift the presser foot, since the feed dogs will pull the fabric under for you. The seam allowance cut edges should align with the seam allowance markings on the serger front, and the seamline should align with the needle(s). It's important to note that the cutting line is not the same as the seamline because of the stitch width.

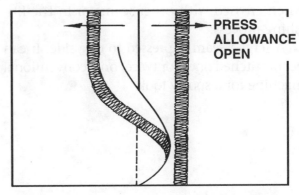

A conventionally stitched seam with a serger finish.

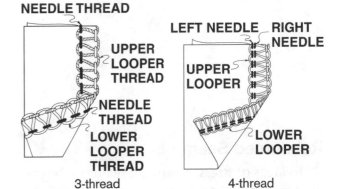

3-thread

4-thread

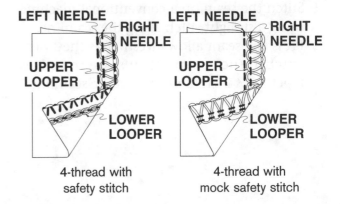

4-thread with safety stitch

4-thread with mock safety stitch

Continued on next page

Serge the seam, carefully guiding the fabric, and sew off the end of the seam for a few inches, creating a chain of thread. (This is called "chaining off.") Then clip the chain, leaving at least a 4-inch (10 cm) thread tail. Do not clip the thread ends next to the fabric since they will be trimmed when crossed with other seams or in the finishing process.

A serged seam is pressed to one side. It can be topstitched once (or twice) on a conventional machine for a sporty look.

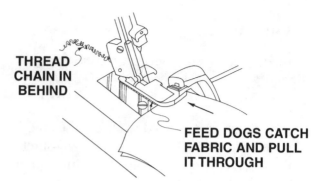

The feed dogs pull the fabric under the presser foot.

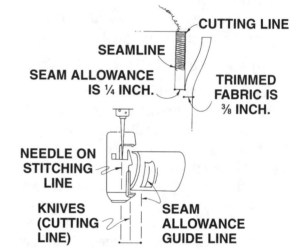

Seamline markings on the front of the serger.

## Reinforced Seam

In areas of stress, a stronger seam can be created by combining the serger and conventional machine. To create a reinforced seam:

1. Stitch the seam on a conventional machine using a straight stitch along the seamline.
2. Press the seam allowances flat as they were stitched (not open), then serge the edges together ⅛ inch (3 mm) from the seamline.

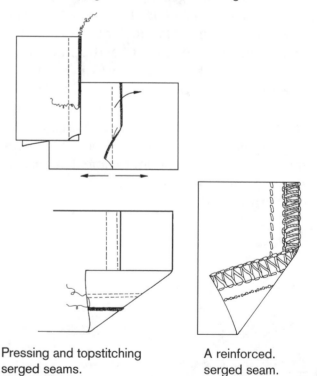

Pressing and topstitching serged seams.

A reinforced serged seam.

Continued on next page

## Flatlocked Seam

Flatlocking is most often used decoratively on the outside of a garment. It does not create a strong seam and should be used in areas of little or no stress. It works best on fabrics that do not ravel.

Because a 3-thread stitch is available on most serger models, the following instructions are for that stitch. Always consult the machine instruction book if you need more specific information.

To set the serger for flatlocking:

1. Adjust the serger for a wide, short- to medium-length stitch. Thread the needle, upper looper, and lower looper.
2. Loosen the needle tension almost completely.
3. Tighten the lower looper tension until that thread forms a straight line along the fabric edge and the needle thread forms a "V" on the fabric underside.
4. Test-serge on fabric scraps until your stitch matches the one in the illustration at the right.

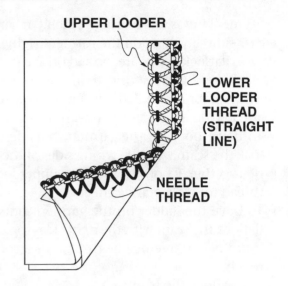

Step 4: A 3-thread flatlocked seam.

Continued on next page

TODAY'S TEEN CONSTRUCTION SKILLS  **67**

Flatlocking is a "reversible stitch," meaning either side can show on the garment right side. As you flatlock, loops are formed on the topside and a ladder stitch is formed on the lower side, once the fabric is pulled flat. Before you sew a seam, decide which side you want to show.

- To have loops on the garment outside, flatlock the seam with the wrong sides of the fabric together. Choose a specialty upper looper thread for a decorative effect.
- To have the ladder on the garment outside, flatlock the seam with the right sides together. Use a decorative needle thread for a special touch.

To flatlock the seam:

1. Determine the desired finished stitch look (see above) and place the fabric layers accordingly.
2. Guide the fabric edges under the serger foot so the stitches hang halfway off the fabric. This allows room for the layers to spread out once the seam is pulled flat.
3. Once the seam is complete, open the fabric layers and gently pull the seam flat.

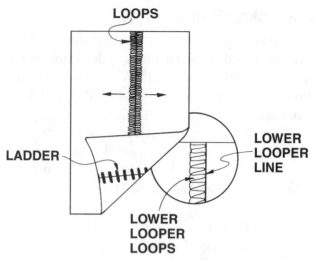

A flatlocked serger seam forms a ladder and loop effect.

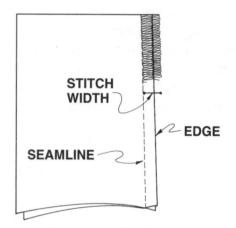

Step 2: Guide the fabric under the serger so the stitches overhang the edge of the fabric.

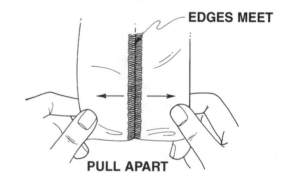

Step 3: Gently pull the seam flat.

## Handout 26

# SECURING SERGER SEAMS

Unlike a conventional sewing machine, the serger cannot backstitch to anchor the stitching. Serger stitching will ravel if it is left unsecured. It's a good idea to leave at least a 4-inch (10 cm) tail of serger chain (stitched serging) at the beginning and end of every seam for anchoring. On many occasions, a seam will be crossed with another seam during construction and it is only necessary to secure the ends of the last seam sewn. When you do need to secure the seam, there are several methods from which to choose.

## Knotting the Threads

The simplest way to secure a serged seam is to simply knot the thread chain close to the end of the seam. This method requires at least a 4-inch (10 cm) thread chain at each end of the seam.

To make a small, inconspicuous knot:
1. Tie the thread chain into a loose knot around a straight pin.
2. Use the straight pin to slide the knot tightly against the fabric edge.
3. Slip the knot to the pin point and pull it tightly to secure.
4. Clip the thread chain close to the knot. For added security, place a small drop of seam sealant on the knot and allow it to dry before cutting the thread ends.

## Applying Seam Sealant

Seam sealant (sometimes called fray-preventer) is a man-made liquid that dries clear and prevents threads from unraveling. Before using it for seam finishing, place a drop of the seam sealant on a scrap of your project fabric and allow it to dry. Check to be sure it doesn't leave a stain; if it does, try another brand. Also, some brands of seam sealant will leave a hard bead when dry, which can be irritating to the skin when you're wearing your garment.

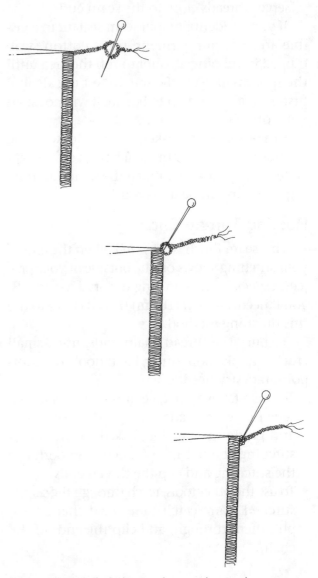

Tying a thread chain into an inconspicuous knot.

Continued on next page

Because only a very small drop of sealant is required to secure the serged seam, it's often easier to use a toothpick or straight pin to apply it rather than trying to control the flow directly out of the bottle.

To use seam sealant to secure the end of a seam:

1. Put a drop onto the threads at the end of the serged seam.
2. Allow the seam sealant to dry completely. This process may take up to 10 minutes. If you can't wait, speed up the process by using a hair dryer or fan!
3. When the sealant is completely dry, clip the serger threads close to the seam ends.

If you accidentally spill seam sealant in a visible area of your garment, use a cotton swab dipped in rubbing alcohol to rub the area until the spot disappears. (Be sure to test the alcohol first on a fabric swatch to be sure it will not stain your fabric!)

In your sewing basket, be sure to keep the seam sealant and machine oil bottles clearly separated—they look very much the same, but mixing them up can be disastrous!

## Burying Thread Ends

This seam finish works well when the end of your stitching shows on the outside of your project, especially when using decorative threads. You'll need a 4-inch (10 cm) thread chain to use this finishing method.

To bury the thread chain ends, use a small crochet hook, loop turner, latch hook, or blunt-point tapestry needle.

• To use a tapestry needle, insert the separated serger chain threads through the needle eye and guide the needle back into the serger stitching about 1 inch (2.5 cm). Smooth out the stitching and clip the thread ends.
• To use the other tools, reach through the serger-stitched seam, catch the thread chain ends, pull them through, and clip the ends of the chain.

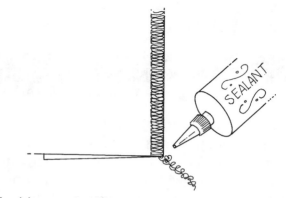

Applying seam sealant.

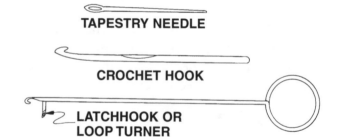

**TAPESTRY NEEDLE**

**CROCHET HOOK**

**LATCHHOOK OR LOOP TURNER**

Loop turner or latch hook.

Anchor the seam end by weaving the chain tail into the seam with a tapestry needle.

Continued on next page

## Machine Securing Threads

This serger anchoring method is fast and easy once you master it, but at first it may seem to be the most difficult. Two techniques are involved —one to anchor the seam beginning, another to anchor the seam end.

- To anchor the *beginning* of the seam: Serge one or two stitches into the fabric edge. Lift the serger presser foot and wrap the thread chain to the front, pulling on it slightly to make it narrower. Place the chain in the seam allowance and serge over it for about 1 inch (2.5 cm) to secure the seam. Clip off the excess chain tail length.

- To anchor the *end* of the seam: Serge one or two stitches beyond the fabric edge and carefully slip the thread chain off the serger's stitch finger. Raise the presser foot and reverse the direction of the fabric so the bulk of the seam is in front of the foot. Lower the presser foot and stitch 1 inch to 2 inches (2.5 cm to 5 cm) over the last stitches in the serged seam, being careful not to cut the previous stitching. (If your serger has a retractable or swing-away knife, this is a good place to use this feature to avoid cutting the previous stitching line.) Chain off (serging off the end of the seam about 4 inches) the seam edge and trim the thread ends.

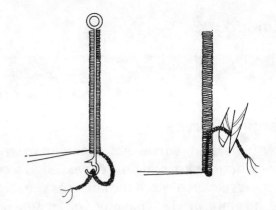

Use a latch hook to pull the chain tail thread through the seam.

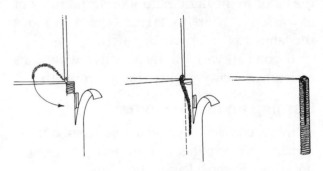

Serging the chain thread tail over the serged seam.

**Handout 27**

# SERGING CORNERS AND CURVES

## Serging Curves

When serging curves, it is important to serge slowly in order to guide the curved edge accurately. It's easier to watch the knives as you serge instead of the needle. That way, you are sure not to trim too much of the fabric and "reshape" your edge. On an outside curve, gradually move the fabric to the right in front of the presser foot as you serge. On an inside curve, gradually move the fabric to the left as you stitch.

If you can vary the serger stitch width, it's easier to sew curves with a narrower width.

## Serging an Inside Corner

Inside corners are easier to serge than outside corners. This technique can be used on slits, square necklines, or serged appliqués.

1. Pretrim the seam allowance from the inside corner before serging. This means you will *not* be trimming away any fabric with the serger knives as you stitch.
2. Serge one inside edge (without trimming away any fabric), and stop when the serger knives are about ½ inch (1.3 cm) from the actual corner. Turn the handwheel to place the serger needle down into the fabric.
3. Raise the presser foot and fold the fabric away from the knife, so the inside corner actually forms a straight line in front of the presser foot. A small tuck will form where the fabric is folded, but will disappear when you return the fabric to its original shape.

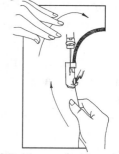

Stitching an outside curve.    Stitching an inside curve.

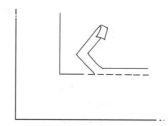

Step 1: Pretrim the seam allowance before stitching an inside corner.

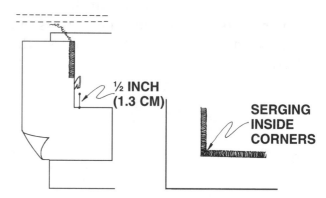

Step 2: Serging the inside corner.

½ INCH (1.3 CM)

SERGING INSIDE CORNERS

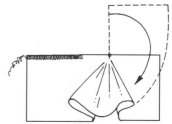

Step 3: Fold the fabric away from the knife to form a straight line.

Continued on next page

4. Lower the presser foot and continue serging the remainder of the edge, being careful not to serge a large tuck into the folded corner, or it may be permanently pleated!

## Serging Outside Corners

The techniques for serging outside corners will be useful for projects like scarves, tablecloths, napkins, and collars as well as decorative serger appliqués.

There are two methods for serging outside corners. One involves serging off one edge and back on to an adjacent edge. The second, more advanced technique involves actually serging *around* a corner.

## Serging Off and On a Corner

Because a serger can form a stitch on or off fabric, completing a corner using this method is easy.

1. Serge one edge of your project and continue off the corner.
2. Pivot the fabric and begin serging again on the adjacent edge.
3. When all edges are complete, secure the corner threads with seam sealant and clip the thread ends when the seam sealant is dry.

## Serging Around a Corner

This method of cornering takes some practice, so don't be discouraged if it doesn't work the first time you try it.

1. Pretrim about 2 inches (5 cm) along the seamline of the adjacent edge you plan to serge, so you'll know exactly where to stitch once you turn the corner.

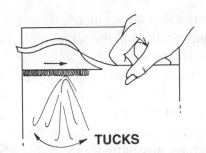
Step 4: Serging the remainder of the inside corner.

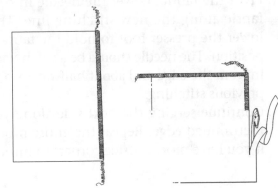
Step 1: Serging off a corner.    Step 2: Pivot and continue serging the adjacent side.

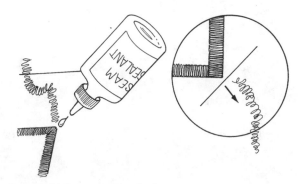
Step 3: Using seam sealant.

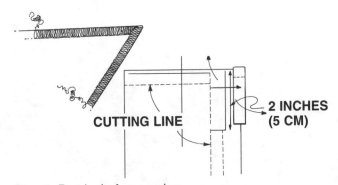
CUTTING LINE    2 INCHES (5 CM)
Step 1: Pretrim before serging.

Continued on next page

2. Serge the first edge and continue off the corner *one* stitch. Stop the serger with the needle out of the fabric.

3. Raise the presser foot, pull a slight amount of slack into the needle thread, and slide the stitches off the stitch finger. Pull the needle thread taut above the tension dials so you don't have any extra loops to distort the corner stitching.

4. Pivot the fabric. Lower the needle into the fabric along the new stitching line. Then lower the presser foot to hold the fabric in position. The needle should be a stitch-width in from the edge and about halfway into the previous stitching.

5. Continue serging the next side along your pretrimmed edge. Repeat the entire process if you have more outside corners to turn.

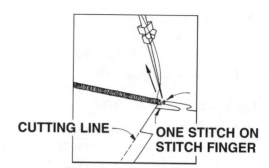

CUTTING LINE — ONE STITCH ON STITCH FINGER

Step 2: Serge one stitch beyond the corner.

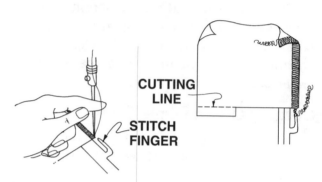

CUTTING LINE

STITCH FINGER

Step 3: Pull a little slack in the needle thread and remove thread from the stitch finger.

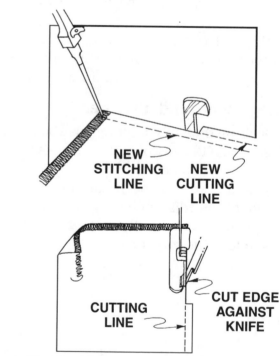

NEW STITCHING LINE    NEW CUTTING LINE

CUTTING LINE    CUT EDGE AGAINST KNIFE

Step 4: Pivot the fabric, reposition the needle, and continue stitching.

**Handout 28**

# SERGING CIRCULAR EDGES

There are two methods for serging in a circle, depending on the finished use. The simplest method, with overlapping stitches, is best used in areas that are not decorative and will not show on your finished project. This lapped stitch method can be used for finishing a turned hem or facing edge, applying ribbing to a T-shirt, or applying a collar to a round neckline. The second method, which takes some practice, is used when the stitching will be visible, such as a placemat edge finish or a decoratively serged neckline edge.

## Lapped Stitch Finishing

1. Serge onto the fabric at an angle.
2. Continue serging around the circle, trimming off the seam allowance as you stitch.
3. When you reach the starting point, overlap the stitching about 1 inch (2.5 cm), trimming your original angled beginning stitches, but not the stitches along your finished edge.
4. Angle the serging off the edge by gradually moving the fabric to the left. Chain off the edge.
5. Put a little seam sealant on the stitching and trim off the chain tail when the seam sealant is dry.

## Finishing Without Overlapping

1. Pretrim along the seamline about 2 inches (5 cm). If you are serging the edges of an oblong or oval placemat, begin and end the stitching along the straight edge.
2. Insert the fabric with the knife against the trimmed edge, and lower the needle into the fabric on the stitching line.
3. Serge around the circle, stopping *exactly* where you began stitching. Turn the handwheel to position the needle out of the fabric.
4. Raise the presser foot and gently pull the fabric behind the needle; chain off about 4 inches (10 cm) without catching the fabric.
5. Thread a blunt-point tapestry needle with the thread chain and work it back through the beginning stitches. Clip the thread tails for a clean finish.

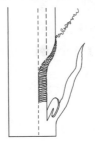

Step 1: Serging onto the fabric at an angle.

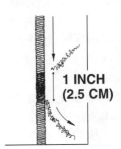

Step 4: Overlap the stitches 1 inch (2.5 cm) and chain off the edge.

**BEGIN SERGING HERE**

2 INCHES (5 CM)

Step 1: Pretrim seam allowance about 2 inches (5 cm) along a straight edge.

**CUTTING LINE**

**STITCHING LINE**

Step 2: Position the machine along the trimmed edge and stitching line.

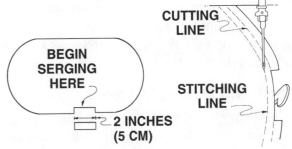

Step 4: Pull the fabric behind the needle and chain off the edge.

Step 5: Weave the thread chain into the stitches.

**Handout 29**

# STABILIZING SERGER SEAMS

Serging is more durable in high-stress areas (such as shoulder seams and pull-over-the-head necklines) when the seams or exposed edges are stabilized to prevent excessive stretching. Some knit fabrics, such as sweater knits and sweatshirt fabric, continue to "grow" if seams aren't stabilized, causing the garment to look oversized and distorted and the seams to pop after the garment is worn a few times. Stabilizing can also produce more uniform stitching on some loosely knit or ribbed fabrics.

Not all knits require this extra care, so test your stretchable fabric. Stretch a small swatch of fabric on the crosswise grain, then release and see if it recovers to its original size and shape. If it does not, one of the following stabilizing options may help your garment look more professional.

## Stabilizing Inside Seams

Here are some methods for stabilizing inside seams:

- Sew a row of straight stitching next to the serged edge finish.
- Serge over narrow ribbon, braid, yarn, or heavy thread, such as buttonhole twist or pearl cotton. To maintain stretch in a serged seam, serge over narrow width of clear elastic, being careful not to cut it with the serger knives.
- Topstitch serged seams in one direction using a conventional straight stitch.
- If your serger offers a chain stitch, use it with an overedge stitch.

## Stabilizing Decorative Edges

Stabilizing single decoratively finished edges often requires means other than those described above to prevent stretching.

- Face the area with matching fabric or fusible interfacing before serging. If your pattern does not offer a facing piece, trace the neckline opening shape of the pattern and create a piece of facing about 2 inches (5 cm) wide. Pin the facing in place and serge.
- Use a separate strip of self-fabric (the garment fabric) under the decorative serging, then trim the excess width close to the stitching.
- Serge over elastic cord, without cutting the cord, and tie the cord ends at the exact length you want. This technique works well for necklines in loosely knit fabrics.

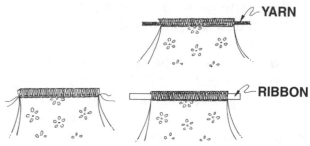

YARN

RIBBON

Stabilizing an inside seam with straight stitching.

Stabilizing an inside seam with ribbon, braid, yarn, or heavy thread.

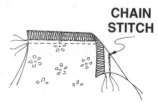

TOPSTITCH SERGED SEAM TO ONE SIDE

CHAIN STITCH

Stabilizing an inside seam with topstitching.

Stabilizing an inside seam with a chain stitch.

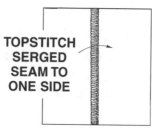

FACING

INTERFACING

SELF-FABRIC STRIP

Serge over a facing or interfacing to stabilize the seam.

Serging over a self-fabric strip.

## Handout 30

# SERGER HEMMING

Using the serger to finish hem edges, whether decorative or functional, gives a professional look to your garment, no matter what the fabric. Serger hemming is fast and fun and can be decorative as well. Be sure to practice each technique before hemming your actual project.

## Serged and Topstitched Hem

A quick finish for any garment hem is to serge-finish the hem edge, turn up the hem allowance, and topstitch it using a conventional sewing machine. Whether your hem is narrow (called a shirt-tail hem) or wider, the serged edge provides a ravel-free finish.

Topstitch a serged hem with a conventional machine using straight, zigzag, or decorative stitches and a single or double needle. To help keep topstitching straight, make a narrow hem and use the edge of your presser foot as a guide for the folded edge.

## Serged Blind Hem

A serger blind hem creates an invisible finish in soft, spongy types of knit fabrics, such as sweatshirting or sweater fabrics. On flat-finish fabrics like denim or T-shirt knits, some stitching may be visible on the right side of the garment.

To create a serged blind hem:

1. Adjust your serger for a flatlock stitch (page 67) at the longest length setting.
2. Press the hem to the garment's wrong side, along the marked hemline. Some bulky fabrics will not hold a crease, so you may need to use pins to hold the hem in place.
3. Fold the hem allowance back toward the garment's right side, with the unfinished hem edge extending about ¼ inch (6 mm) to the right.
4. Serge on the unfinished hem edge so that the needle *barely* catches the folded edge. If you used pins to hold the hem in place, be sure they clear the serger knives to avoid severely damaging the serger (and you!). As you come back to the stitching starting point, chain off the serged edge and clip the threads.

5. Remove any pins and open the hem. Pull the stitching line flat and press the hem.

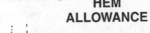
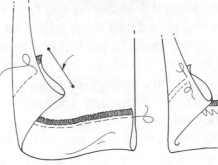
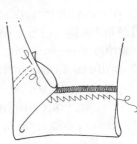

Serger hem finish with a single topstitched line.

Serger hem finish with a double needle topstitched hem.

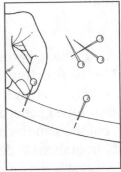

Step 2: If necessary, pin the hem to hold it in place.

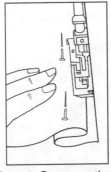

Step 4: Serge on the unfinished hem edge

Step 5: Pull the stitching line flat and press.

Continued on next page

## Flatlocked Hem

A flatlocked hem is often found on sportswear, such as sweatshirts, T-shirts, or jogging suits. The serger stitching is visible on the right side of the garment hemline and can be sewn with a decorative thread for even more design prominence.

To create a flatlocked hem:

1. Adjust the serger for flatlock stitching (page 67).
2. Press the hem allowance to the garment's wrong side. Fold the same width to the wrong side a second time, catching the raw hem edge in the second fold. Secure the hem in place with pins placed near the first hem fold.
3. Flatlock over the second folded edge, *without trimming any fabric.* If you can turn the serger knife to a noncutting position, this is a good place to do so. Be sure to catch the raw hem edge in your stitching.
4. As you come back to the starting point, do not overlap the stitches—just chain off the folded edge. To anchor the thread ends, pull them to the wrong side and tie off.
5. Open the hem and pull the stitching flat. Press the hemline to set the stitches.

## Rolled Hem

A narrow rolled edge creates a decorative hemline suitable for finishing any light- to medium-weight fabric. You may be familiar with commercially sewn rolled hems on napkin and placemat edges, but the same techniques can be used on garments, from sheers to denims to wools.

The fabric edge actually rolls under because the stitch width is narrower than the space between the serger needle and the knives. When used with decorative thread, the rolled hem can create the look of a narrow binding.

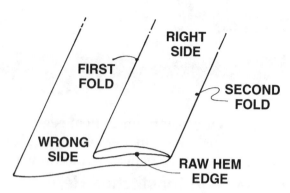

Step 2: Fold the hem twice for flatlocking.

Step 3: Flatlock over the second folded edge.

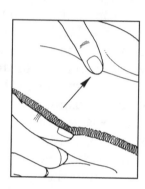

Step 5: Pull the stitching flat and press the hem.

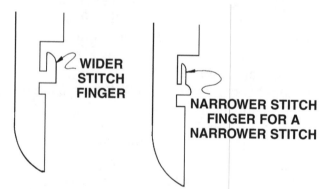

Step 1: Narrow and wide stitch fingers.

Continued on next page

To create a rolled hem:

1. Adjust the serger to a rolled hem setting. Each machine requires different adjustments to do rolled hemming, so consult your manual. Make the following changes in the normal serger settings:
- Use a narrower stitch finger.
- Use a rolled hem presser foot, if needed.
- Use only the right needle position.
- Use a narrower stitch width and cutting width.
- Use a shorter, satin-stitch length.
- Tighten the lower looper tension to produce a rolled-under edge.

2. Trim the garment hem allowance to ½ inch (1.3 cm).

3. Serge along the hemline with the garment right side up, trimming off the excess as you stitch. It's important to stitch smoothly and evenly since this is the edge that will show on the finished garment.

4. As you come back to the starting point, stop stitching where you began and chain off. Secure the thread ends with seam sealant and trim off.

   To create a lettuce edge on knit fabrics or ribbing, stretch the hem edge as much as you can while roll hemming. When the knit is relaxed, it will create a decorative rippled effect.

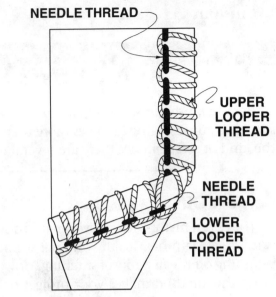

Step 1: Rolled hem edge.

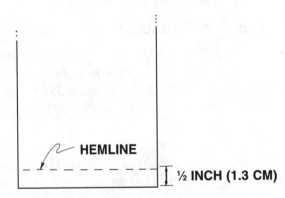

Step 2: Trimming the garment hem.

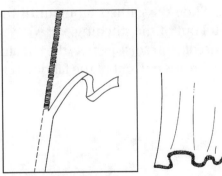

Step 3: Serge along the hemline, trimming away excess fabric.

Lettuce edging.

**Handout 31**

# REMOVING SERGER STITCHING

Removing serger stitching can be a very frustrating experience! Unlike conventional machine stitching, most serging involves more than two threads, making the task even harder. Depending on the kind of serger stitch, there are several methods of removing stitches from which to choose.

## Serge It Off!

The easiest method to remove serging mistakes is to serge again next to the original seamline, trimming off the first row of stitching. However, using this method makes your project or garment *smaller* than it was originally, so it won't work in all situations.

## Pull the Thread(s)

An easy way to remove serger stitching without trimming off fabric is to pull the needle thread(s). Depending on the kind of serger stitch to be removed, there may be one or two needle threads to pull.

1. Clip off one end of the seam thread chain and smooth out the thread tails on the other end. The shortest thread(s) will be the needle thread(s).

2. Gently pull the needle thread(s) to gather up the fabric. Slide the gathers along until the threads pull out of the stitching.

3. Once the needle thread(s) are free, the remaining looper threads pull out of the fabric freely.

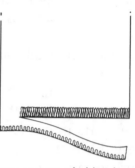

One way to remove serger stitching is to serge off the first row of stitching.

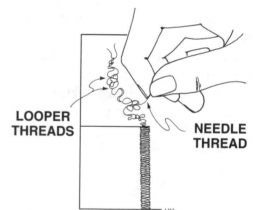

Step 1: Smooth out the thread tail and grab hold of the needle thread.

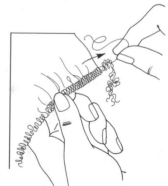

Step 2: Gently pull the needle thread to pull out stitching.

Continued on next page

## Use a Seam Ripper

On 3- or 3/4-thread serging mistakes use a seam ripper for quick stitch removal. A seam ripper often comes with your serger or conventional sewing machine tools.

- Slide the seam ripper under the loops on one side of the stitching, and carefully cut through the threads for the length needed. With the looper threads cut, the remaining threads will pull free. The remaining messy thread bits can be picked up by running the sticky side of masking or cellophane tape over the seamline.

## Unravel Chain Stitching

Have you ever struggled trying to open a bag of dog food sewn with an industrial chain stitch? A serger chain stitch can be equally frustrating until you find the right thread to pull—then it will simply unravel.

Some sergers produce a chain stitch separate from the overedge portion of the stitch; others incorporate it as part of the edge finishing. To unravel a chain stitch:

1. Clip the chain close to the fabric at the *end* (the beginning won't work) of the serger stitching line.
2. On the backside of the seam, separate the threads with a pin.
3. Pull on the looper thread and the chain stitch will pull out without any effort.

Seam ripper.

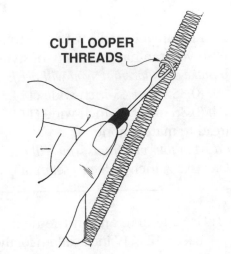

Cut the looper threads with the seam ripper for easy removal.

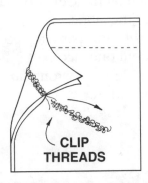

Step 1: Clip the thread chain at the *end* of the stitching line.

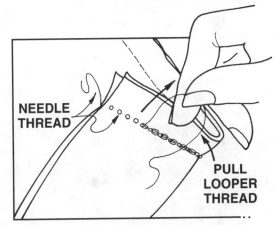

Step 3: Pull the looper thread to unravel the chain stitch.

Name_____ Date _____ Class_____

# PLACEMAT

Brighten up your table with a festive placemat for any occasion. A placemat is quick and easy to make, so you can have a variety of styles for everyday and all your favorite occasions.

*To make one placemat\* you will need:*
- ⅜ yd. (0.35 m) of 45-inch-wide (114.5 cm) fabric
- ⅜ yd. (0.35 m) of 45-inch-wide (114.5 cm) polyester fleece
- Thread to match fabric

*\* For a set of four placemats, you will need 1½ yds. of fabric.*

   *Note:* Use ⅝-inch (1.5 cm) seam allowances.

**Step 1:** Use the diagram on the next page to make a 12 × 17-inch pattern for the placemat. Fold the fabric in half lengthwise with selvages together. Pin the pattern to the fabric. Cut two placemat pieces from the fabric.

**Step 2:** Pin the same pattern piece to the fleece. Cut out one piece.

**Step 3:** Baste fleece to wrong side of one placemat section.

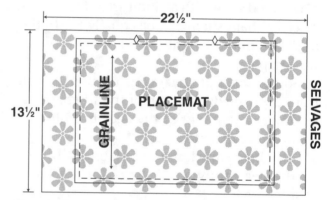

Step 1: Cutting placemat from fabric.

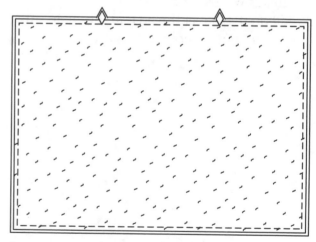

Step 3: Baste fleece to wrong side of one placemat section.

Continued on next page

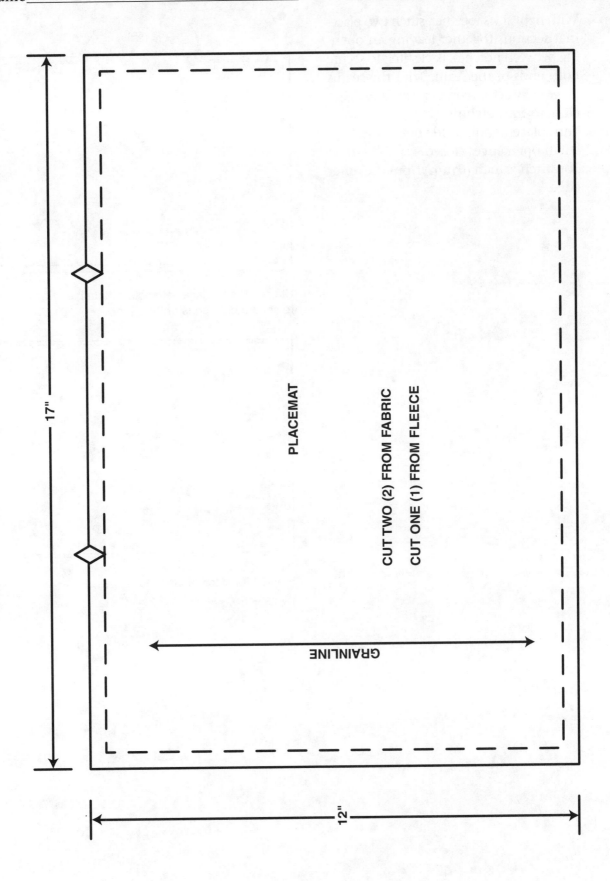

PLACEMAT

CUT TWO (2) FROM FABRIC

CUT ONE (1) FROM FLEECE

GRAINLINE

17"

12"

Continued on next page

TODAY'S TEEN CONSTRUCTION SKILLS **83**

**Step 4:** With right sides together, stitch two place-mat sections together leaving an opening between notches. Backstitch to secure both ends of the seam. Trim the seams diagonally across corners. Trim the fleece close to the stitching.

**Step 5:** Turn placemat right side out. Press. Slip-stitch open edges closed.

**Step 6:** Topstitch ¼ inch (6 mm) from the outer edge.

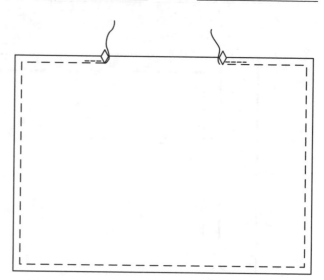

Step 4: Stitch placemat sections together. Backstitch to secure both ends of the seam.

Step 6: Topstitch along outer edges.

**Handout 33**

# EYEGLASS CASE

If you need a place to keep your glasses or sunglasses, you may want to make two—one for yourself and one for a grandparent or older friend.

*You will need:*
- One 8 × 16-inch (20.5 × 40.5 cm) piece of quilted fabric
- Optional: Appliqué or decorative trim of your choice
- Thread to match fabric

**Step 1:** Trace the pattern for the eyeglass case. Fold a piece of 8½ × 11-inch paper in half. Place the pattern on the fold of the paper. Cut out the full-sized pattern. Fold fabric in half to form a square. Cut two of the case pattern pieces from the fabric. Transfer markings with chalk.

**Step 2:** Attach the appliqué(s) or decorative trim as indicated on pattern, by hand-stitching, or follow package directions. This piece is now the **outer case**. The other fabric square is the lining.

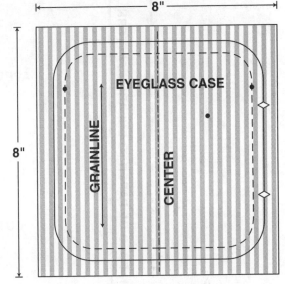

Step 1: Cut two case pieces from fabric.

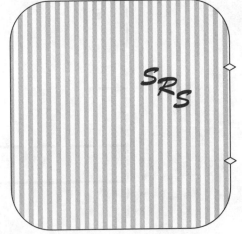

Step 2: Attach the appliqué(s) or decorative trim as indicated on pattern.

Continued on next page

# Eyeglass Pattern

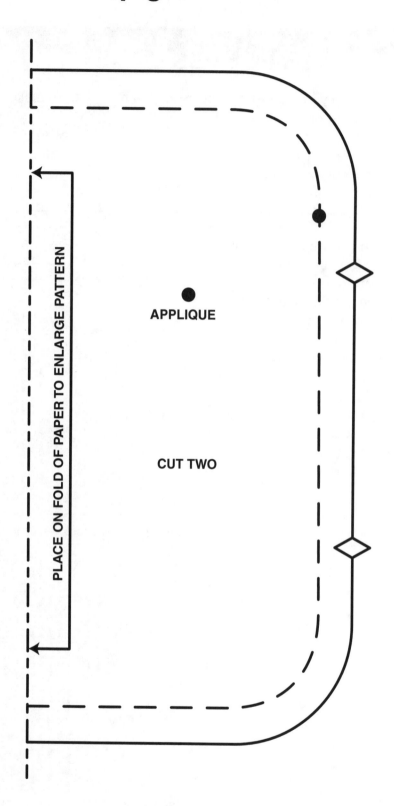

PLACE ON FOLD OF PAPER TO ENLARGE PATTERN

APPLIQUE

CUT TWO

Continued on next page

**Step 3:** With right sides together, stitch lining and outer case pieces together using a ⅜-inch (1 cm) seam allowance. Backstitch to secure both ends of the seam. Leave an opening between notches for turning.

**Step 4:** Grade seam allowances by cutting layers at different widths close to stitching. Clip curves. Be careful not to clip through the stitching.

**Step 5:** Turn case right side out. Slipstitch opening closed. Press. Topstitch around entire square about ⅛ inch (3 mm) from the edges.

**Step 6:** Fold case in half so the appliqué or trim is visible. Match dots, pin, and make sure edges are even. Stitch edges together below the large dot, about ¼ inch (6 mm) from the edge. Backstitch to secure both ends of the seam.

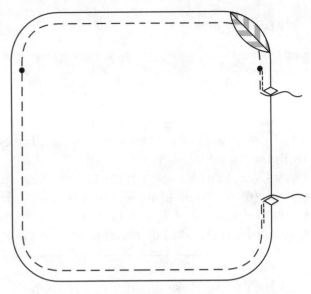

Step 3: Stitch outer case and lining piece together.

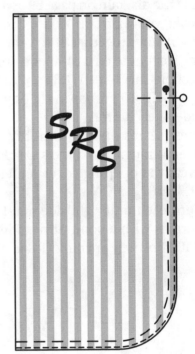

Step 4: Fold case so finished edges are together, and stitch close to edge.

**Handout 34**

# CASEROLE CARRIER

Transport casseroles and cakes to picnics and potlucks with ease in this clever carrier. Designed for a 13-by-9-inch (33-by-23 cm) oblong pan, the quilted-cotton tote also helps keep hot dishes hot.

*You will need:*

- ¾ yd. (68.5 cm) of 45-inch (114.5 cm) wide single-face prequilted fabric
- ¾ yd. (68.5 cm) of 45-inch (114.5 cm) wide lining fabric (cotton to go with the quilted fabric)
- 1 yard (91.5 cm) of ⅜-inch (1 cm) wide grosgrain ribbon
- Two ½-inch (1.3 cm) diameter dowels, each 16 inches (40.5 cm) long

**Step 1:** Cut one of each pattern piece A and B from the quilted fabric and the lining. Use the diagram on page 89 as a guide to make your pattern.

**Step 2:** Right sides together, stitch the two lining sections to their corresponding quilted sections in a ½-inch (1.3 cm) seam. Leave a 4-inch (10 cm) opening on one long side of each unit.

**Step 3:** Press seams open to simplify pressing after turning. Trim corners to reduce bulk. Press the opening edges under ½ inch (1.3 cm).

**Step 4:** Turn each unit right side out. Push out corners with a point turner. Press edges flat. Slipstitch opening closed.

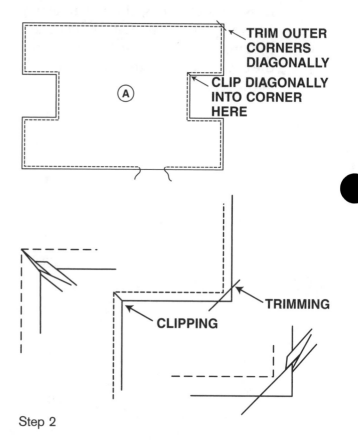

Step 2

Continued on next page

Name_____ Date _____ Class_____

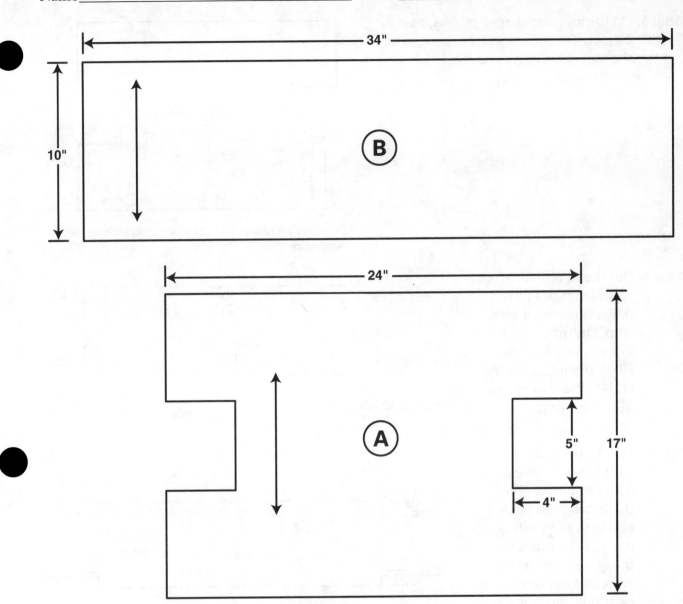

Step 1

Continued on next page

**Step 5:** On the irregular-shaped piece A, turn in 1⅛ inch (2.8 cm) toward the lining along the four short edges and stitch.

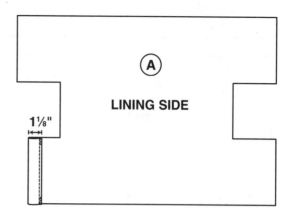

Step 5: Turn under 1⅛", then edgestitch along the inner edge.

**Step 6:** Cut the ribbon into four equal lengths. Press under one end of each strip. On the quilted side of piece B, satin stitch the turned-under ends in place as shown in the drawing.

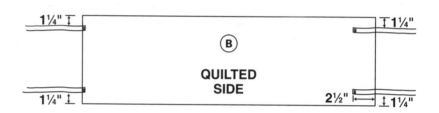

Step 6: Attach ribbons.

**Step 7:** Lay the irregular unit with the right side down on a flat surface. Place the rectangular piece, also with right side down, perpendicular to the other with the same amount extending over each side. Pin along the edges to hold the layers together. Mark stitching lines on the rectangle to make a box 8" by 11" (20.5 by 28 cm). Stitch through all thicknesses.

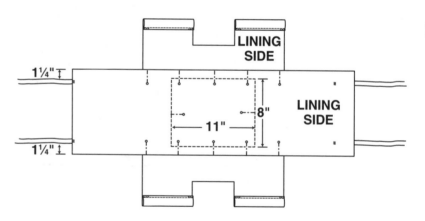

Step 7: Pin and stitch parts A and B together.

**Step 8:** Insert dowels into the casings to form handles. To use, lay out the carrier right side down and set the pan in the center. Bring the ribbon ends together over the pan and tie. Bring up the handle edges and carry the casserole securely.

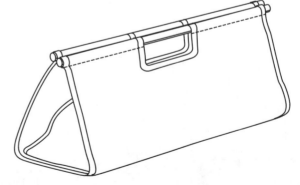

Step 8: Finished casserole carrier.

## Handout 35

# LAUNDRY BAG

Choose a bath towel in your favorite color to stitch up into this handy drawstring bag. The outside pocket, made from a washcloth, is ideal for keeping handwashables separate. The laundry bag can be made from a variety of fabrics, but the towels' prefinished edges eliminate the need for seam and edge finishing.

*You will need:*
- One bath towel
- One washcloth to match or coordinate (or two washcloths for two pockets)
- 1 package of wide single-fold bias tape
- 1 pair of 54-inch-long (137 cm) shoelaces in a color to coordinate with towel

**Step 1:** Right sides together, fold the towel in half crosswise. Place the washcloth in the desired position for the pocket; pin to upper towel layer only. (Repeat on the other side of the bag if a second pocket is desired.) Open out the towel and edge-stitch the washcloth in place on three sides.

**Step 2:** Refold the towel with the pocket to the inside. At the sides measure 2 inches (5 cm) down from the top and mark a 1¼-inch-long (3.2 cm) casing opening. Pin and stitch the sides in ⅝-inch (1.5 cm) seams, leaving the seam unstitched at the casing opening. Backstitch at beginning and end of stitching to secure.

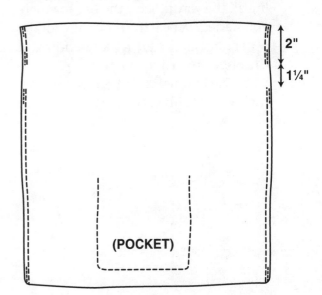

Step 2: Allow for a 1¼-inch (3.2 cm) opening in the side seams, 2 inches (5 cm) from the top.

Continued on next page

**Step 3:** In the unstitched seam area, fingerpress the seam allowances open and stitch them flat.

**Step 4:** Measure the width of the bag from one side seam to the other. Cut two strips of bias tape to match this measurement, plus ½ inch (1.3 cm). Press under ¼ inch (6 mm) on each end. Pin each tape strip in place 2 inches (5 cm) down from the top, beginning and ending at the seam openings. Stitch close to the long edges. Do not stitch the ends. Turn the bag to the right side.

**Step 5:** Knot one end of one shoelace and fasten a safety pin to the other end. Thread the pinned end through one casing opening all the way around the bag to where you started. Repeat the procedure for the other shoelace, starting and ending at the opposite casing opening.

**Step 6:** Untie the knotted ends, then tie together the two ends on each side.

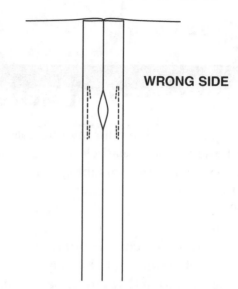

WRONG SIDE

Step 3: In the unstitched seam area, open the seam allowances and stitch them flat to the bag.

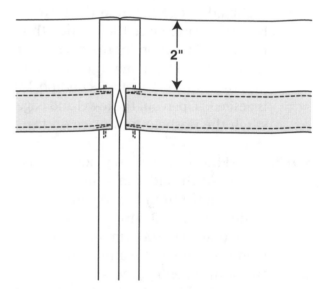

2"

Step 4: Stitch bias tape in place 2 inches (5 cm) from the top, beginning and ending at seam openings.

Step 6: Finished laundry bag.

## Handout 36

# CHEF'S APRON

This simple apron has three handy pockets and ties long enough to wrap around and tie in front, so the chef can tuck a towel in the waist.

*You will need:*

- 1 yd. (0.95 m) of 45-inch (114.5 cm) medium- to heavy-weight cotton blend fabric
- Two 3 yd. (5.5 m) packages of extra-wide, double-fold bias tape
- Thread to match fabric
- One pair of ½-inch-wide D-rings

**Step 1:** Fold the fabric in half lengthwise with the selvages together. At one end, measure across the fabric 13 inches (33 cm) from the fold and mark with chalk or washable marker. Measure and mark the fabric the same way at the other end and at the center. Use a yardstick to connect the marks with a straight line. The fabric from the fold to the line will be the apron itself.

**Step 2:** To mark the "bib" of the apron: At one end, measure 6 inches (15 cm) across from the fold and mark. Measure down the side of the apron 11 inches (28 cm) and mark that point. Using a measuring stick, extend the markings into the apron until they meet. Use a dinner plate as a pattern for a curve and place it so the edges of the plate touch the straight lines. Mark around the plate to make a curved line that meets the straight lines on each side of the plate.

**Step 3:** Mark the 15-inch-wide (38 cm) pocket as shown on the cutting layout. Cut out the apron and the pocket (only one pocket is needed).

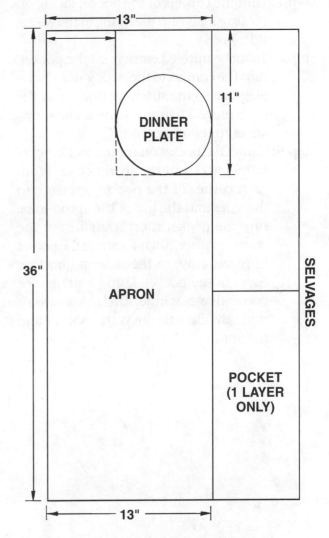

Steps 1-3: Marking and cutting out the apron.

Continued on next page

**Step 4:** To hem the sides of the apron, turn the edges under ¼ inch (6 mm), then turn under ¼ inch (6 mm) again. Press. Stitch each hem close to the turned-under edge.

**Step 5:** Hem the top and bottom edges of the apron the same way as in Step 4, except turn the edges under 1 inch (2.5 cm) each time. Press and stitch.

**Step 6:** On the pocket, turn down the selvage edge 1 inch (2.5 cm) toward the right side to make the pocket facing. Press. Stitch the ends of the facing in place ⅝ inch (1.5 cm) from the edge. Stitch ⅝ inch (1.5 cm) from the edge on three sides of the pocket to form a guideline for pressing.

**Step 7:** Trim the corners of the pocket facing on the diagonal. Turn the facing to the wrong side. Press.

**Step 8:** To make mitered corners on the pocket, turn the corners to the wrong side on the diagonal so the stitching lines meet the fold; press. Then press the seam allowances to the wrong side.

**Step 9:** Center the pocket on the apron 12 inches (30.5 cm) from the lower edge. From each corner of the pocket, measure to the sides and the top of the apron to be sure the pocket is on straight. Pin the pocket in place. Then topstitch the pocket in place, close to the side and bottom edges of the pocket. Using a straight or decorative machine stitch, sew two or more dividers through the pocket and the apron.

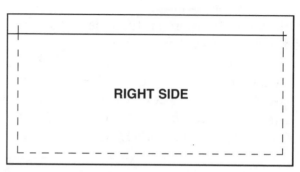

Step 6: Turn the pocket facing down 1 inch (2.5 cm) and stitch ⅝ inch (1.5 cm) from the edge on three sides.

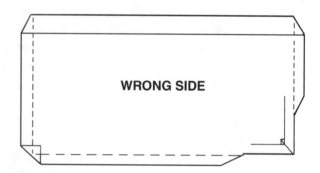

Step 8: Turn corner to wrong side so stitching lines meet; press. Press seam allowances to wrong side along the stitching line.

Continued on next page

**Step 10:** Cut one piece of bias tape 2¼ yd. (2.10 m) long and one piece 1½ yd. (1.40 m) long. Notice the tape has a wider and a narrower side. Place the wider side of each tape to the wrong side of the apron bib. Allow one yard (0.95 m) of each tape to hang free at the base of the bib for the waist ties. Then pin the tape onto each side of the bib. The other free end (the free end at the top of the bib) of the longer (2¼ yd. or 2.10 m) tape will form the neck strap. With the apron right side up, stitch the entire length of each tape close to the turned-under edge of the tape.

**Step 11:** The short end of the 1½ yd. (1.40 m) tape should extend 1½ inches (3.8 cm) above the apron bib; cut off any excess. Slip this end into the D-rings. Turn the tape end under, then stitch it down at the apron bib corner. Turn under the other three tape ends ¼ inch (6 mm), then turn them under again the same amount. Stitch to secure. Slip the end of the neck strap through the center of both D-rings from the front of the apron to the back; adjust the neck strap to the desired length and hold in place securely; then put the end of the neck strap over the top of the D-ring closer to the back of the apron and under the second D-ring. Pull the end of the neck strap to lock the strap in place.

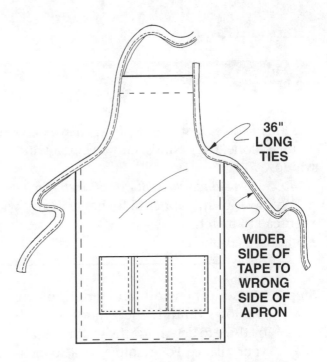

36" LONG TIES

WIDER SIDE OF TAPE TO WRONG SIDE OF APRON

Step 10: Along the sides of the bib, place the wider side of the bias tape to the wrong side of the apron and pin. Stitch the entire length of the tape as directed.

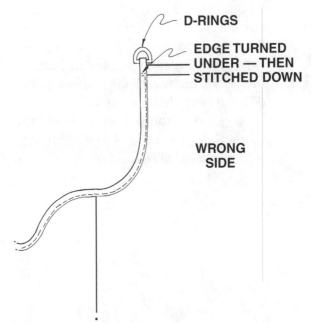

D-RINGS

EDGE TURNED UNDER — THEN STITCHED DOWN

WRONG SIDE

Step 11: Slip the D-rings onto the tape at the apron bib. Fold the tape under and stitch in place as directed.

## Handout **37**

# WINDOW VALANCE

One of the easiest and least expensive decorating tricks you can use is a window valance. It can be used alone, over blinds, curtains, or a window shade. You can make a valance to fit almost any window.

*To make a valance for a 30- by 60-inch window, you will need:*
- 1½ yds. (140 cm) fabric, 45 inches (115 cm) wide
- Thread to match
- Standard curtain rod

**Step 1:** Measure the width and length of the window. Multiply the window's width by three to determine the width to make your valance. For example, for a 30-inch-wide (76 cm) window, you would want a valance that is 90 inches wide (228 cm).

**Step 2:** Your valance should cover no more than ⅓ of the window length. Measure the length of the window. Divide it by three. For a 60-inch (152 cm) window, your desired valance length would be 20 inches (51 cm) in finished length. To that figure, add 7 inches (18 cm). Three inches (7.5 cm) will be allowed for the casing (also called a "rod pocket") to hold the curtain rod; the other 4 inches (10 cm) is for the hem allowance.

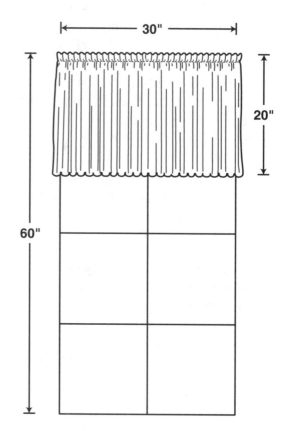

Step 2: A valance should cover no more than ⅓ of a window.

Continued on next page

**Step 3:** Fold the fabric, selvages together. Measure 27 inches (68.5 cm) down from the cut edge. Draw a straight line across the fabric using a fabric marker or chalk. Cut along this line. You will have two pieces of fabric, each 27 by 45 inches.

**Step 4:** Place the right sides of fabric together along the selvage, and stitch the two pieces together with a ⅝-inch (1.5 cm) seam. Backstitch to secure the seam at both ends. Press seam open. Finish the side hems (the remaining two selvage edges) of the valance. First, fold the selvage edges under ¼ inch (6 mm) and press. Then fold the edges under again ¾ inch (2 cm), press and pin in place. Machine stitch the side hems close to the inner folded edge, removing the pins as you sew. Backstitch to secure stitching. (See Handout 19 on page 50).

**Step 5:** Measure and pin a 3-inch (7.5 cm) hem at the top edge of the valance. Press. Fold the inner edge under ¼ inch (6 mm) as you did in Step 4 and pin in place. Machine stitch the hem ⅛ inch (3 mm) from the inner folded edge. Measure down 1 inch from the top edge of the valance. Using chalk or a fabric marker, mark a line 1 inch from the top edge. Stitch along the marked line, backstitching at the beginning and end. This second row of stitching forms a casing, or the "rod pocket," in which to insert the curtain rod. The rod pocket will be 1¾ inches (4.5 cm) deep.

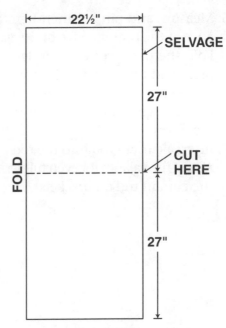

Step 3: Layout and cut the fabric.

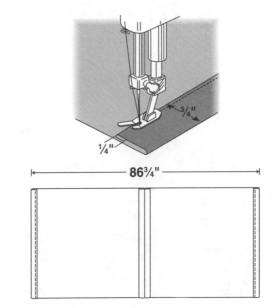

Step 4: Hem the sides of the valance.

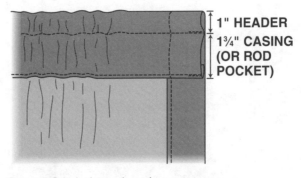

Step 5: Stitch the rod pocket.

Continued on next page

**Step 6:** Measure and pin a 4-inch hem allowance at the bottom edge of the valance. Fold the inner cut edge under ¼ inch, press and pin in place. Machine stitch the hem ⅛ inch (3 mm) from the inner folded edge. Backstitch to secure stitching. Press.

**Step 7:** Insert a curtain rod into the rod pocket. Adjust the valance for even fullness. Place the curtain rod on brackets.

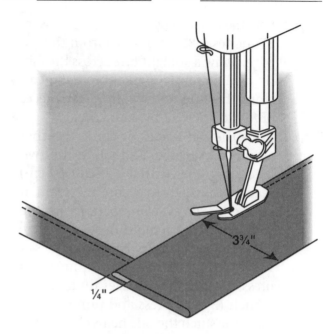

Step 6: Stitch a 3¾-inch hem.

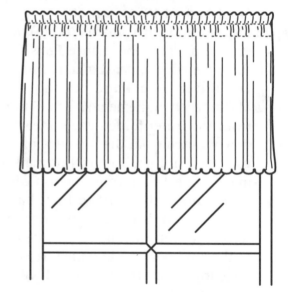

Step 7: Adjust the fullness and mount the valance.

Name_____ Date _____ Class_____

# PILLOW WITH BUTTON OPENING

You can't beat throw pillows for adding pizzazz to almost any room. Your fabric choice is practically limitless. For textural interest, consider faux fur, corduroy or fleece—or recycle your old denim jeans!

*To make a pillow with lapped opening for a 14-inch form:*
- ½ yd. (.5 m) of 45-inch (114.5 cm) wide fabric, or denim from one pair of jeans
- Two strips of fusible interfacing, each 1½-by-16 inches (3.8 by 40.5 cm)
- One 14-inch (35.5 cm) pillow form
- Three ¾-inch (2 cm) buttons

**Step 1:** For pillow front, cut two pieces, each 10¼-by-16 inches (26 by 40.5 cm). Cut one piece 16-inches ( 40.5 cm) square for pillow back.

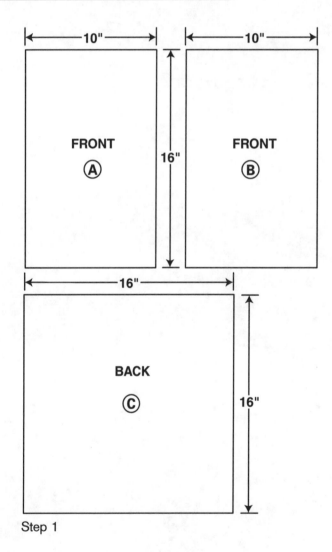

Step 1

Continued on next page

**Step 2:** Fuse an interfacing strip on the wrong side of one long edge of each pillow front section. Serge-finish or zigzag-finish the long interfaced edges.

**Step 3:** Press under 1½ inches (3.8 cm) on each interfaced edge. Edgestitch the fold and topstitch 1⅜ inches (3.5 cm) from the folded edge. On one front section, evenly space markings for three buttonholes. Stitch buttonholes.

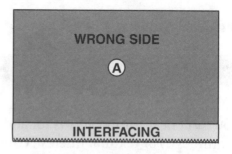

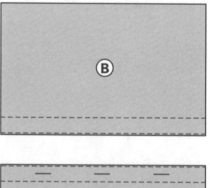

Step 2: Fuse interfacing on the pillow front sections and serge-finish or zigzag-finish the edges.

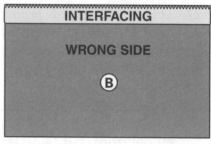

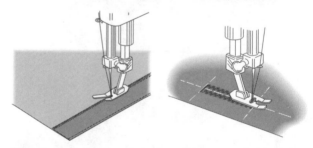

Step 3: Press under the serged edges and edgestitch and topstitch the folded edges. Mark and stitch the buttonholes according to machine directions.

Continued on next page

**Step 4:** Lap the buttonhole section 1⅜ inches (3.5 cm) over the other section. Baste in place at the sides.

**Step 5:** Right sides together, stitch pillow front unit to pillow back in a ½-inch (1.3 cm) seam. Trim corners diagonally and grade seams to reduce bulk. Press seams open to simplify pressing after turning. Turn pillow to the right side and push out corners with a point turner. Press edges flat.

**Step 6:** Insert pillow form through the button opening. Mark placement for buttons under buttonholes. Hand stitch buttons in place.

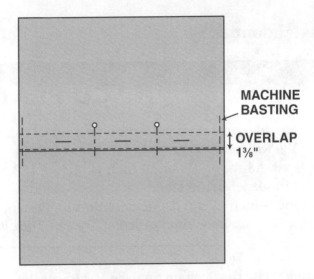

MACHINE BASTING

OVERLAP 1⅜"

Step 4: Lap the buttonhole front section 1½ inches (3.8 cm) over the other front section. Baste at the sides.

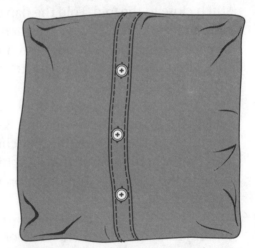

Step 6: Finished pillow with button opening.

**Handout 39**

# CD PLAYER TOTE

Provide some extra protection for your CD player as you tote it along hands-free in this great bag.
*You will need:*
• ½ yd. (.5 m) of 45- or 60-inch (114.5 or 152.5 cm) wide ravel-free fabric, such as felt, fleece or Ultrasuede® brand fabric
• One ¾-inch (2 cm) diameter button (optional)
*[Note: Vary size as necessary to fit the CD player. These instructions are for a 5½-by-5-inch (14 by 12.5 cm) player.]*

**Step 1:** Use the diagram on page 103 to cut the fabric sections for the tote. Mark the folds with chalk or erasable marker.

**Step 2:** Fold the bag section on Fold 1. Edgestitch close to the fold. Fold the flap section on its fold line. Begin edgestitching one long edge, pivot to edgestitch the fold, then pivot again to edgestitch the other long edge.

**Step 3:** Pin the flap unstitched edges on the bag folded edge as shown in the drawing. Begin stitching the flap on the side, matching previous stitching. Continue stitching close to the cut edges and finish on the opposite side.

**Step 4:** Turn the unit over and stitch ¼ inch (6 mm) from the edgestitched fold of the bag.

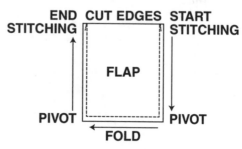

Step 2: Fold and edgestitch flap.

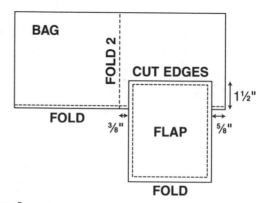

Step 3

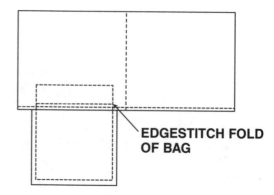

Step 4
Continued on next page

**102** TODAY'S TEEN CONSTRUCTION SKILLS

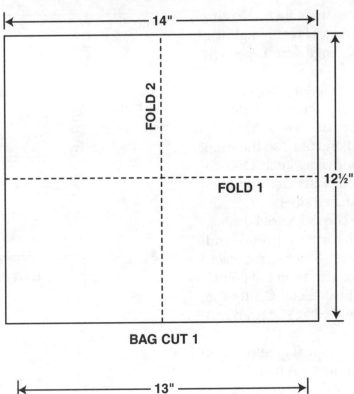

**BAG CUT 1**

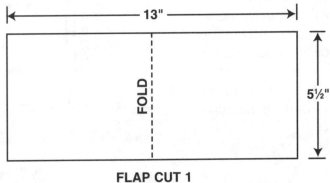

**FLAP CUT 1**

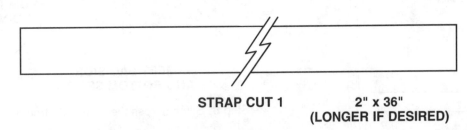

**STRAP CUT 1**    **2" x 36"**
**(LONGER IF DESIRED)**

Step 1: Follow the measurements above to create the pattern pieces for your **CD-Player Tote**. Mark the folds with chalk or an erasable marker.

Continued on next page

**Step 5:** For the strap, press in ½ inch (1.3 cm) along one long edge. Press remaining strap width in half lengthwise. Edgestitch both long edges.

**Step 6:** Center one strap end on the bag's Fold 2, even with the flap placement. Stitch in a box and "X" formation to secure.

**Step 7:** Fold the bag unit on Fold 2 so the strap and flap are to the inside. Stitch a ¼-inch (6 mm) seam through all four thicknesses on the two unstitched sides.

**Step 8:** To square off the corners, refold the bag diagonally at each corner so the side and bottom seams meet. Stitch across each corner ⅝ inch (1.5 cm) from the point.

**Step 9:** Turn the bag right side out. Center the loose strap end on the bag side seam and stitch in place.

**Step 10:** (Optional) Open out flap and mark buttonhole placement ¾ inch (2 cm) from the edge. With the machine set for a short stitch length, stitch a box ⅛-inch (3 mm) wide by ⅞-inch (2.2 cm) long. Cut a single slash the length of the box. Mark button placement on the bag opposite the buttonhole. Stitch the button in place.

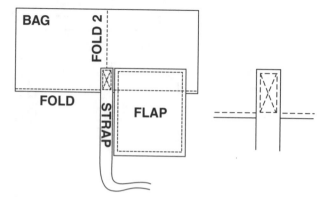

Step 6

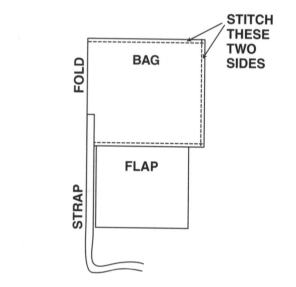

Step 7

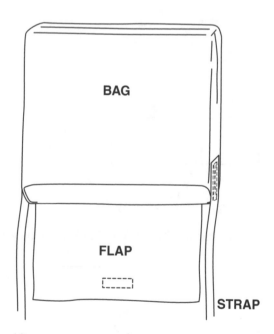

Step 10

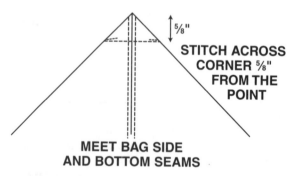

Step 8: Stitch across the corner ⅝" from the point.

## Handout **40**

# POLARFLEECE® MUFFLER AND MITTENS

Chase away winter chills with a colorful fringed muffler and mittens to match. You can make the mittens to fit any size, so the set makes a great gift, too.

*You will need:*

- ⅝-yard (.60 m) of 60-inch (152.5 cm) wide fleece
- ½ yard (.50 m) of ¼-inch (6 mm) wide elastic

**Step 1:** Cut a 9-inch (23 cm) wide strip across the fabric width—60-inches (152.5 cm) long.

**Step 2:** Using a fabric marker or chalk, mark a line 5 inches (12.5 cm) from each end of the strip. Then slash to the line every ⅜ inch.

**Step 3:** Turn under ⅜ inch (1 cm) on each long edge and stitch a narrow hem.

**Step 4:** Make your mitten pattern from your own hand. With your fingers together and your thumb in a relaxed position, trace around your hand on tissue paper. Mark the wrist. Add ½-inch (1.3 cm) plus a ⅝-inch (1.5 cm) seam allowance around the entire hand, rounding out the area over the fingers. At the wrist, extend the cutting and stitching lines straight down 3 inches (7.5 cm), perpendicular to the wrist line.

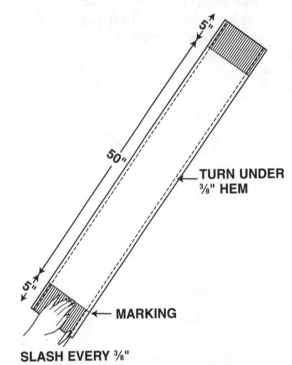

**TURN UNDER** ⅜" HEM

**MARKING**

**SLASH EVERY** ⅜"

Steps 2 and 3

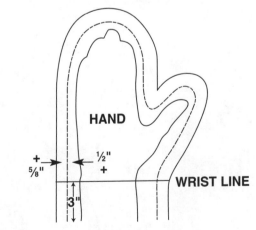

**HAND**

⅝" ½"

**WRIST LINE**

3"

Step 4

Continued on next page

**Step 5:** Lay out the fleece single layer. Use your mitten pattern to cut four shapes with the fabric stretch going around the mitten. Reverse the pattern for one side of each mitten. On each piece, mark the wrist line. Chalk-mark each shape on the "wrong" side to avoid shading variances in the fleece. If it's difficult to determine the right side, choose a side and use it consistently.

**Step 6:** Measure your wrist and cut two elastic strips this measurement plus 2½ inches (6.5 cm). Cut each piece in half, making four strips. Zigzag one elastic strip to the wrong side of each mitten half at the wrist marking, stretching the elastic to fit as you sew.

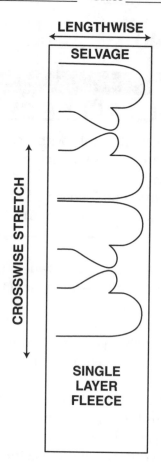

Step 5: Reverse the mitten pattern to make corresponding mitten pairs.

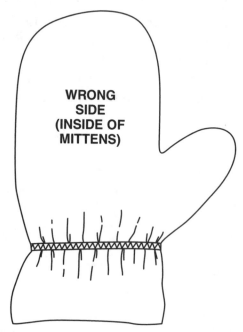

Step 6: Stretch elastic and stitch to mitten along wristline.

Continued on next page

**Step 7:** Right sides together, pin two mitten halves together and straight stitch a ⅝ inch (1.5 cm) seam. Stitch again ⅛ inch (3 mm) from the seamline within the seam allowance. Trim seam allowances close to stitching. Repeat for the remaining mitten halves.

**Step 8:** Turn under and stitch a ¼-inch (6 mm) hem on the unfinished edge. Turn mittens to the right side.

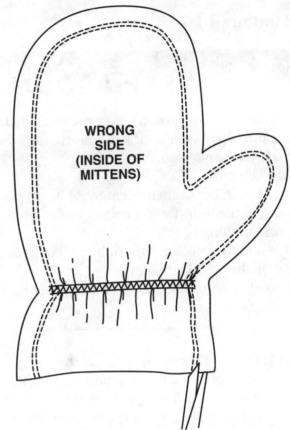

**WRONG SIDE (INSIDE OF MITTENS)**

Step 7: Stitch together two mitten halves, and trim seam allowances close to stitching.

**Handout 41**

# WRAP-AROUND WRIST WALLET

When your clothes don't have pockets, whether you're biking, rollerblading, or out for a walk, it's difficult to carry your door key. This handy wrist wallet solves that problem. There's room for keys and a little money, too.

*You will need:*

- One 4-inch by 9½-inch (9 cm by 24.3 cm) piece and one 2¾-inch by 9½-inch (7.1 cm by 24.3 cm) piece of medium-weight cotton blend fabric for wallet. (For men, make each piece 10½ inches [26.3 cm] long.)
- One 4-inch by 9½-inch (9 cm by 24.3 cm) piece of terry cloth lining (For men, the piece should be 10½ inches [26.3 cm] long.)
- ¼ yd. (0.25 m) of hook-and-loop fastener tape
- One glue stick

**Step 1:** Press the narrow strip (2¾ inch [7.1 cm] wide) of cotton blend fabric in half lengthwise. Cut a 5¾-inch (14.6 cm) strip of hook-and-loop fastener tape (the remaining hook-and-loop tape will be used in Step 5); cut both sections of this tape in half lengthwise. Rub the back of the "loop" section with the glue stick and center it next to the fold of the fabric strip and stick it in place. Machine stitch the tape in place on the long sides only.

**Step 2:** Press under ¼ inch (6 mm) on one long edge of the larger cotton blend piece: then press under another ½ inch (1.3 cm). Rub the back of the "hook" section of the narrow fastener tape with the glue stick; center it along the lengthwise fold in the fabric and stick it in place. Stitch around the fastener tape along all sides.

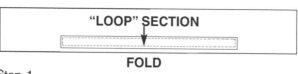

Step 1

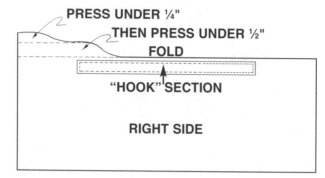

Step 2

Continued on next page

**Step 3:** Fasten the two fabric pieces together by aligning the hook-and-loop tape sections. Curve this wallet strip around your wrist to preshape it and to lessen the rippling of the fastener tape. Remove the wallet strip from your wrist and pin the ends together as they lie, maintaining the curve. Stitch the narrow (2¾ inch [7.1 cm] wide) fabric strip to the wider fabric piece by extending the topstitching rows (created in Step 1 when the hook-and-loop tape was applied) to the ends of the "wallet."

**Step 4:** With right sides together, pin the wallet piece to the terry cloth lining. Stitch around the wallet in a ¾-inch (6 mm) seam. Trim the corners, grade the seam allowances, turn the wallet and press. (Refer to Handout 10 on page 27.)

**Step 5:** With cotton side up, use the glue stick on the back of the "hook" section of the remaining wide fastener tape and stick the fastener tape on one end of the wallet. Glue the "loop" section of the fastener tape and place it close to the edges on the terry cloth side at the opposite end of the wallet. With the cotton blend side up, topstitch ¼ inch (6 mm) from all the edges of the wallet, catching the outer edge of both sections of the fastener tape in the stitching. Stitch down the remaining unstitched edge of the "hook" section. (The "loop" section remains unstitched on one edge.)

**SLIGHT BULGE**

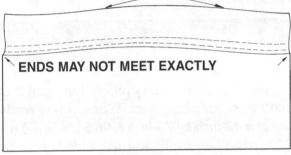

**ENDS MAY NOT MEET EXACTLY**

Step 3

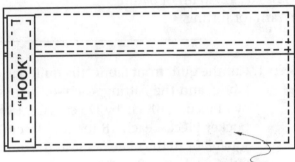

**"LOOP" SECTION ATTACHED TO TERRY CLOTH LINING UNDERNEATH**

Step 5

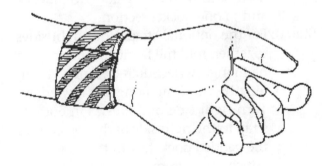

Wrist Wallet

## Handout 42

# CONVERTIBLE PILLOW/QUILT

Folded up, it's a comfy pillow, but open it up and this ingenious pillow turns into a twin-size quilt that's ideal for sleep-overs. When you're ready to pack it up, just fold it back into a pillow and go!

*For a 42-inch by 70-inch (106.5 cm by 170 cm) quilt, you will need:*

- 2⅝ yds. (2.40 m) of 45-inch-wide (114.5 cm) cotton blend fabric for the quilt front and pocket. (You will need 2¾ yds. [2.55 m] if you want the optional strap.)
- 2 yds. (1.85 m) of coordinating fabric for the quilt back
- 2⅝ yds. (2.40 m) of batting
- Yarn for tufting

**Step 1:** Cut the quilt front fabric, the quilt back fabric, and the batting, each 43 inches by 71 inches (109 cm by 175 cm). Cut two pocket pieces, each 18 inches (46 cm) square, from the same fabric as the quilt front, and one 18-inch square from the batting. Cut the strap piece, 38 inches by 5 inches (96.5 cm by 12.5 cm), from the quilt front fabric (optional).

**Step 2:** Baste batting to wrong side of quilt back and to one pocket section.

**Step 3:** For the optional strap: With right sides together, fold the fabric for the strap in half lengthwise. Stitch a ⅜ inch (1 cm) lengthwise seam along the raw edges. Turn right side out. Press. Pin ends of strap to the right side of the top edge of the padded pocket, with the strap folds ¾ inch (2 cm) from the pocket sides. Baste the strap in place. Pin strap away from seam allowances.

**Step 4:** With right sides together, pin other pocket section to the padded pocket. (If you are including the strap, sandwich it between the pocket layers.)

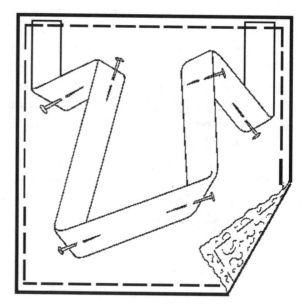

Step 3: Pinning the strap in place on the pocket.

Continued on next page

Stitch the pocket upper and side edges only (leaving the bottom of the pocket open for turning right side out) in a ⅜-inch (1 cm) seam. Trim the corners diagonally. Trim the batting close to stitching. Turn right side out. Press. Topstitch ¼ inch (6 mm) from upper edge through all thicknesses.

**Step 5:** Mark five positions for tufts on pocket. Arrange the tufts evenly near each corner and at the center. Thread a large needle with a single strand of yarn about 20 inches (51 cm) long. At each mark, take a ¼-inch (6 mm) stitch through all layers, leaving a 1-inch (2.5 cm) tail at both the beginning and the ending point of the stitch. Cut the yarn, and repeat this tufting process at each mark. Tie each tail in a double knot.

**Step 6:** Fold the quilt back and the pocket in half lengthwise to find the center fold. Mark the center fold on the bottom of the pocket and one end of the quilt back using a pin or a washable marker. With the tufted side of the pocket up (the side on which the tufts are tied), pin pocket to quilt back, matching the centers. Topstitch the pocket in place ¼ inch (6 mm) from the finished side edges of pocket. Baste lower pocket and quilt back edges together.

**Step 7:** With right sides together, stitch quilt front to quilt back using a ½-inch (1.3 cm) seam. Leave a 10-inch (25.5 cm) opening along one lengthwise side of the quilt for turning the quilt right side out. Trim corners diagonally. Trim batting close to the stitching. Turn right side out. Press the seams flat along the edges of the quilt. Slipstitch the 10-inch (25.5 cm) opening edges together. From the quilt front, topstitch ¼ inch (6 mm) from the finished edges through all thicknesses.

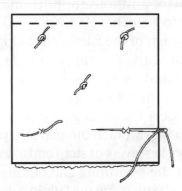

Step 5: Making tufts on the pocket.

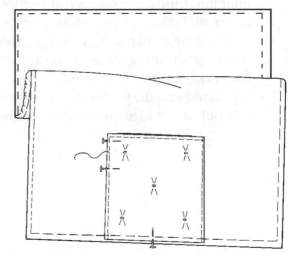

Step 6: Pinning the pocket to the quilt back.

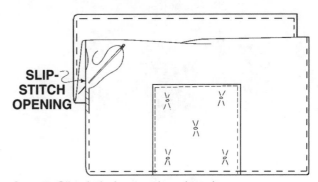

Step 7: Slipstitch the opening closed.

Continued on next page

**Step 8:** Mark positions for tufts on quilt front 6 to 10 inches (15 to 25.5 cm) apart. The design of the fabric may help you determine the positions. Stagger the rows. Thread a large needle with a single strand of yarn. Working from the quilt front, repeat the tufting process as described in Step 5. Stitch through all layers (except pocket layers or strap ends), leaving tails at the beginning and ending points of each stitch. Tie the tails in a double knot.

**Step 9:** To fold quilt: With quilt front up, fold quilt into thirds, one side over the other, using side edges of pocket as a guide. Then fold quilt in quarters from the top down, positioning all layers on top of the pocket section. To form pillow, insert your hand into the pocket and turn right side out over folded quilt. Poke out corners and shape as necessary into a pillow.

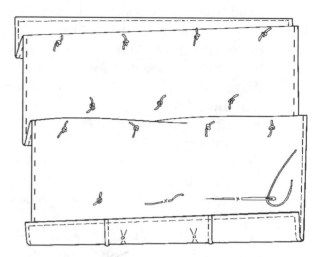

Step 8: Mark tuft positions, stitch through all layers, and tie tails as directed.

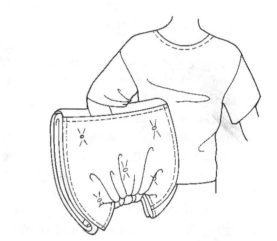

Step 9: Folding the quilt into the pillow.